MOZART, BEETHOVEN, SCHUBERT

Dietrich von Hildebrand

MOZART, BEETHOVEN, SCHUBERT

Dietrich von Hildebrand

Translated by John Henry Crosby

Foreword by Manfred Honeck

HILDEBRAND
PROJECT

Originally published in German as *Mozart, Beethoven, Schubert.*
Regensburg: Josef Habbel, 1962.

First English translation published 2024 by Hildbrand Project, 1235 University Blvd. Steubenville, OH 43952

Copyright © 2025 Dietrich von Hildebrand Legacy Project
All rights reserved

Cataloguing-in-Publication Information
Von Hildebrand, Dietrich, 1889–1977 | Honeck, Manfred, foreword author | Crosby, John Henry, translator. Mozart, Beethoven, Schubert / by Dietrich von Hildebrand ; foreword by Manfred Honeck ; translated by John Henry Crosby.— First English Edition. Includes bibliographical references, appendix, and index. | Steubenville, OH: Hildebrand Press, 2025.
ISBN 978-1-939773-23-4
Subjects: LCSH: Music—Philosophy and aesthetics. | Mozart, Wolfgang Amadeus, 1756–1791—Criticism and interpretation. | Beethoven, Ludwig van, 1770–1827—Criticism and interpretation. | Schubert, Franz, 1797–1828—Criticism and interpretation. | BISAC: MUSIC / History & Criticism | PHILOSOPHY / Aesthetics | MUSIC / Individual Composer & Musician
Classification: LCC ML3845.H55 2024 | DDC 781.17—dc23

Typeset by Kachergis Book Design
Set in Adobe Caslon

Cover Design by Marylouise McGraw George

Cover Image: Violinist in the Belfry Window by Edward von Steinle
Image Source: Public Domain. Painting in the Städel Museum, Frankfurt am Main

Front Cover Font: Circular Bold by Laurenz Brunner

Produced by Christopher T. Haley

www.hildebrandproject.org

*In caritate Christi
delectissimis
Bertae et Gualterio Braunfels*

*This English translation
is dedicated in loving memory of
Madeleine F. Stebbins*

Contents

Foreword by Manfred Honeck xix

Translator's Preface by John Henry Crosby xxi

Wolfgang Amadeus Mozart 1

Ludwig van Beethoven 23

Franz Schubert 43

Appendix: Additional Writing on Music 69
    i. "Sacred Music" from *Aesthetics, vol. 2* 69
    ii. "Beethoven on *Fidelio*" from *Aesthetics, vol. 2* 77
    iii. "Richard Wagner" from *Aesthetics, vol. 2* 82
    iv. Selections from the unpublished essay on Richard Wagner 86
    v. "Verdi" from *Aesthetics, vol. 2* 95

Index 99

Index of Names 103

Index of Musical Works 107

Dietrich von Hildebrand

Dietrich von Hildebrand was born in Florence in 1889, and studied philosophy under Adolf Reinach, Max Scheler, and Edmund Husserl. He was received into the Catholic Church in 1914. He distinguished himself with many publications in moral philosophy, in social philosophy, in the philosophy of the interpersonal, and in aesthetics. He taught in Munich, Vienna, and New York. In the 1930s, he was one of the strongest voices in Europe against Nazism. He died in New Rochelle, NY in 1977.

Hildebrand Project

We advance the rich tradition of Christian personalism, especially as developed by Dietrich von Hildebrand and Karol Wojtyla (Pope St. John Paul II), in the service of intellectual and cultural renewal.

Our publications, academic programs, and public events introduce the great personalist thinkers and witnesses of the twentieth century. Animated by a heightened sense of the mystery and dignity of the human person, they developed a personalism that sheds new light on freedom and conscience, the religious transcendence of the person, the relationship between individual and community, the love between man and woman, and the life-giving power of beauty. We connect their vision of the human person with the great traditions of Western and Christian thought, and draw from their personalism in addressing the deepest needs and aspirations of our contemporaries. For more information, please visit: www.hildebrandproject.org

Editorial Board

General Editor: John F. Crosby*
Franciscan University of Steubenville

Rémi Brague
University of Paris, Sorbonne, Emeritus
Romano Guardini Chair of Philosophy,
Ludwig Maximilian University of Munich, Emeritus

Rocco Buttiglione
John Paul II Chair for Philosophy and History of European Institutions
Pontifical Lateran University

Antonio Calcagno
King's University College at The University of Western Ontario

Hanna-Barbara Gerl-Falkovitz
Technische Universität Dresden, Emerita Hochschule Heiligenkreuz

* Student of Dietrich von Hildebrand

EDITORIAL BOARD

Dana Gioia
Judge Widney Professor of Poetry and Public Culture
University of Southern California

John Haldane
University of St. Andrews
Baylor University

Alice von Hildebrand[*†]
Widow of Dietrich von Hildebrand

Joseph Koterski, SJ[†]
Fordham University

Sir Roger Scruton[†]
Writer and Philosopher

Josef Seifert[*]
Edith Stein Institute of Philosophy, Granada, Spain

D. C. Schindler
Pontifical John Paul II Institute for Studies on Marriage and Family
Washington, DC

Christoph Cardinal Schönborn
Archbishop Emeritus of Vienna

Fritz Wenisch[*†]
University of Rhode Island

[*] Student of Dietrich von Hildebrand
[†] Deceased

Special Thanks

SINCE THIS VOLUME contains some of the Hildebrand Project's very first translations of Dietrich von Hildebrand into English, we gratefully acknowledge our donors who have generously enabled us to present many of Hildebrand's works to the world, with more still to come.

EXTRAORDINARY SUPPORT

Howard and Roberta Ahmanson • Taylor and Caroline Butterworth • Madeline L. Cottrell • Cushman Foundation • Donald and Michele D'Amour • Sean Fieler • Geoff and Lauren Gentile • Dana Gioia • Frank and Sally Hanna • Nicholas and Jane Healy • Alice von Hildebrand† • Robert L. Luddy • Patricia C. Lynch† • Lee J. Matherne • Thomas and Suzanne Murphy† • James and Mary Perry • Duncan C. Sahner • John Studzinski CBE • Scott and Lannette Turicchi

† Deceased

PATRONS

Scott and Martha Blandford • Hedy K. Boelte • Budnik Family Foundation • Daniel and Teresa Cotter • John and Pia Crosby • Michael and Suzanne Doherty • Peter Flanigan Memorial Fund • Rose-Marie Fox-Shanahan • Mary G. Georgopulos • Edward and Alice Ann Grayson • Julia Harrison • Barbara B. Henkels • Daniel and Anne Hill • Richard and Vera Hough • Robert Kreppel • Vincenzo and Caitlin La Ruffa • Peter Lawrence • Thomas and Mara Lehrman • Prince Rupert Loewenstein[†] • H. Kimberly Lukens • Franco S. Madan • Charles A. Mastronardi Foundation • Colin Moran • Emilie Murphy-Nimocks • Stephen and Jeanne Pavela • Jeffrey[†] and Mary Petrino • Tim and Martha Reichert • Charles Scribner III • Robert[†] and Joan Smith • R. Templeton Smith Foundation • Madeleine F. Stebbins[†] • Stanley Stillman • Jules and Katie van Schaijik • Gregory C. Woodward

BENEFACTORS

Joshua Bailey • Doug Brown • Dana Marie Buchanan • H.Em. Raymond Leo Cardinal Burke • John F. Cannon • Michael and Meghan Caponiti • Charterhouse of the Transfiguration Carthusian Monastery • Allison Coates and Joshua Knuebuhl • Sheila A. Conforti • Phil Damiani • Myles Harrington • Patrick Hart[†] • Fr. Adam Hertzfeld • Roy and Elizabeth Heyne • John K. Hicks • Martín von Hildebrand • Manfred Honeck • Robert D. Hurt • Michael C. Jordan[†] • Timothy and Nancy Joyce • Paulette Kardos • John Kelly • Aloysius Ju Hyeok Kim • Matthew and Veronica Leonard • The Rafael Madan and Lilian Casas Foundation • Judy Mead • Judy A. Miles • Kathryn M. Missert • Brian and Juliane Mogck • William and Robin Mureiko • Elaine C. Murphy[†] • Therese O'Brien • Kevin and Dawn O'Scannlain • Fr. James Puglis, TOR • Mauricio Roman • William H. Rooney • Timothy and Judy Rudderow • Jonathan and Rebecca Sanford • Daniel and Annie Schreck

† Deceased

SPECIAL THANKS

• Fr. Thomas W. Shaw • Roy and Patricia Sheetz • Stan Sienkiewicz • Fr. Zachary Swantek • Richard† and Rose Tondra • Richard and Margaret Wall • Katherine Weir • Fritz K. Wenisch†

FRIENDS

Amanda Achtman • Fr. Ryan J. Adams • James D. Arden • Roy Barkley • James Beauregard • Edwin and Pat Bercier • Stafford Betty • Steven and Stephanie Block • Fr. John Boyle • Emily E. Brammer • Shannon Cagnina • Julia Calinescu • Andrew Cannon • Ellen A. Carney • Paul and Dianne Check • Daniel J. Cheely • Ronda Chervin • Marion A. Clauss† • Joshua Cole • John Paul Cotter • Carol Cuddeback • Susan F. Dane • Cheryl Daye • Fr. Albert J. DeGiacomo • Douglas and Leni Dewey • Nicole C. Ehred • Norma Ehrenberg • Taylor J. Elzner • Maria Fedoryka • John and Claire† Foster • Paul M. and Jane L. Frank • Fr. Andrew Fryml • Arthur and Mariluz Giron† • Rabbi Mark Gottlieb • Willard and Shirley Haley • Fr. David Hammond • Karen Hanley • John Hanson • James A. Harold • Philip J. Harold • Tonita M. Helton • Jo-Ann M. Henry • Michelle Hillaert • Linda Holleran • Neal J. Howard • Thomas Howard† • John Iverson • Timothy Jaeger • Dolores S. Jarrell • Patrick Jobst • Shannon A. Joseph • Douglas Keck • Elizabeth R. Kelly • Joseph Kruger • Christopher Lacaria • Louise Lamb • Jake Lang • Ron Ledek • Robert Levine • John Linn • John H. Linnartz • Marcel and Susan Lipkowitz • Ryan K. Lovett • Alasdair MacIntyre† • Joline Mann • Daniel Mark • Fr. Francis Martin† • Marie E. Martin • Brent McAdam • Laura McCormick • Marylouise McGraw • Matthew McKowen • Marie Cabaud Meaney • Nora L. Metzler • Michael and Rebecca Matheson Miller • Douglas Minson • Gerard and Germana Mitchell • Roberta De Monticelli • James F. Morgan • Robert S. Mortenson Jr. • Dennis B. Mulcare • Ronald and Lucy Muller • Beatrice Murgio • Barbara P. Murphy • Fr. Gerald E. Murray • Bernarda A. Neal • Thomas and Mary Nightengale • Deacon George Nolan • Andrew and Barbara Parrish •

† Deceased

Barbara C. Quintal • Dan Rasmussen • Bartolomé Ribas Ozonas and Elisabeth Wannieck Sattler • Britt and Noah Riner • Rosemary Rodriguez • Carl and Sharon Rudorf • Mark Ryland • Barbara Sanders • Javier Sanz Latiesas • Joyce Schaeffer • Ann Schmalstieg Barrett • Kathleen C. Schmiedicke • Fr. Fabian Schneider • Stephen D. Schwarz • Fr. Robert F. Slesinski • Abigail Spence • Zeb and Christie Stearns • Timothy and Louise Stebbins • Stephanie Stoeckl • Raymond and Virginia St. Pierre • Martha A. Sullivan • Jonathan and Julie Teichert • Joan Thomas • Erik and Anne Tozzi • Susan Treacy • Kathleen Tuthill • Fr. Jon Tveit • Larry A. Vaclavik • JWM van Keeken • Tom Venzor • Ada Vergne • Fr. Walter Wagner, OP • Bernard Wenisch • Kent and Nancy Young • Monica Zarandona

Foreword

By Manfred Honeck

THIS LITTLE BOOK IS A TREASURE, not only because it discusses three of the greatest composers, but also because the author is willing actually to engage with their music. It does not claim to be a modern musicological treatise. Rather, it invites one to listen closely so as to gain a deeper understanding of the music and its composers within the overall beauty of creation. This approach makes Dietrich von Hildebrand's consideration of the works of Mozart, Beethoven, and Schubert something extraordinary and special.

The honesty with which the author ventures to speak of the great masters is also captivating. His conclusions are not influenced by clichés and the opinions of his time. He is committed only to what is revealed in the music, guided by a conscience that strives for God. Now this does not mean that everyone must come to the same conclusions, but in the search for the true, the good and the beautiful, a genuine, fruitful dialogue can emerge from different points of view.

Let me take a brief look at the three composers myself, as I have been privileged to know them in my life as a musician.

With Mozart, beauty always shines; despite harmonic boldness and much drama, he never goes off the rails. He seems to understand human emotions like no one else, and he can capture them musically in a compelling way. He is both humanly and musically credible. Yet his music remains mysterious. He who composed so effortlessly, allows his melodies, which always seem right, to fit into the whole with simplicity. He remains for me probably the most brilliant of the composers.

Beethoven is a revolutionary; he looks briefly to heaven, but first wants to remake the world. No one has notated so many *sforzati*: he shocks, sets new accents, and cares not about conventions. With him there are new standards, because he develops or intensifies the motif technique. With him, small motifs become whole movements, as for example in the famous Fate Motif of the Fifth Symphony. He was also someone who struggled to form his themes, as his notebooks attest. Here we encounter a master of variety the likes of which we have never seen since.

Though all three of the composers worked in Vienna, Schubert is the only one who was also born there. He lacks the renown and internationality that Mozart and Beethoven experienced through travel. In his themes we wander through loneliness, abandonment, longing, love, pain and death. He seems to be a bit lost in the world, not wanting to change it much either. His music is created for a small circle of friends; he is poor and has hardly any support from influential people. He speaks the language of the middle class—in his case Viennese—and captures the Viennese mentality in its *Gemütlichkeit* and melancholy. But those who mistake his approachability for ordinariness are mistaken: his genius unfolds from the seemingly ordinary, even as he prepares a dwelling for heaven.

These brief thoughts are intended to help the reader become attuned to Dietrich von Hildebrand's rich and profound reflections. This will succeed best if the object to be contemplated is always before our eyes (or better, in our ears): the inimitable music of the three masters, which reveals something new with each new encounter, because what it reveals contains an unfathomable reflection of the glory of the Creator.

Manfred Honeck is music director of the Pittsburgh Symphony Orchestra and known internationally for his acclaimed performances and Grammy-winning recordings.

Translator's Preface

By John Henry Crosby

THE LONG-AWAITED PUBLICATION of this English translation of Dietrich von Hildebrand's *Mozart, Beethoven, Schubert* marks not just the arrival of a gem of musical appreciation, but also the work without which the Hildebrand Project might never have been established.

As a young violinist at a summer music festival in 1996, I made my first attempt at translating Hildebrand with his essay on Mozart. Little did I know that this translation would be a prelude of what was to come years later when I founded the Hildebrand Project in 2004. These essays spoke to me powerfully as a young musician, because they gave expression and new meaning to the love, reverence, and gratitude I felt so deeply for these great composers. In the intervening years, and most recently in preparing them for this English edition, Hildebrand's essays have lost none of their original power to fascinate and move me; in fact, they strike me as deeper and more potent today than they did all those years ago.

Mozart, Beethoven, Schubert first appeared in German in 1962 (Regensburg: Josef Habbel). "Mozart" and "Schubert" likely originated as lectures. "Beethoven" exists in a shorter, earlier version in Hildebrand's collection of essays *Die Menschheit am Scheideweg*, which appeared in 1954. Before that, "Beethoven" appeared in a smaller predecessor volume to *Die Menschheit am Scheideweg* called *Zeitliches im Lichte des Ewigen* published in 1932 (Regensburg: Josef Habbel). Even prior to that, in 1929, "Beethoven" appeared, almost certainly for the first time, in a German publication called *Der katholische Gedanke*; it is not certain whether it had originally been intended as a speech. In translating "Beethoven" for the present volume, I carefully compared the 1954 and 1962 versions. While the 1954 text contains passages not included in the 1962 version, I chose to translate the 1962 version because Hildebrand had cut and consolidated certain lengthy passages from the 1954 edition and because he had added important new passages to the 1962 text.

All three essays were delivered publicly as talks in 1953, 1954, and 1955 for the Austrian Institute in New York City. "Mozart" was later given in Salzburg in 1956 (whether in an identical form as it exists in *Mozart, Beethoven, Schubert* is uncertain), under the title "Mozart: Geist und Botschaft" (Mozart: Spirit and Message). Fittingly, this presentation included a "musical portion," with four choral works of Mozart performed as part of the event.

Preparing this volume, it seemed to me only natural to include Hildebrand's writings on other composers. His only other major such text is on Richard Wagner, written at the end of his life and left unpublished. The Wagner essay is in fact longer than any of the essays in *Mozart, Beethoven, Schubert* and in part fragmentary. I have translated selections from the more finished portions of the essay in which the reader will encounter Hildebrand's vision of Wagner's music as a whole and also his interpretation of several Wagnerian operas.

Given the ties between the Hildebrand and Wagner families and Dietrich von Hildebrand's passion for Wagner's music, some additional context seems in order. Wagner had died (1883) by the time Dietrich von Hildebrand was born (1889), but he had been a frequent guest at San Francesco, the Hildebrand family villa in Florence. Wagner's widow, Cosima, was a close friend of both Dietrich's parents. In 1906, she invited the sixteen-year-old Hildebrand to attend the festival in Bayreuth, the

Wagnerian mecca even to this day, where Wagner had built an opera house specifically suited to the performance of his works.

Two letters from Cosima to Hildebrand's parents, both dated July 12, 1906, provide a rare early impression of the young man. "Dietrich has conquered all hearts here at Wahnfried," Cosima wrote to Adolf von Hildebrand. "I waited up to greet him, but soon had to retire because of an unfortunate cold. From afar I heard much laughter, and so hope that his first evening here was a happy one."[1] To Irene von Hildebrand, Cosima had this to say: "For his sake I was especially happy to overrule the fairly firm prohibition on attending rehearsals, for he has a very special nature. His fervor, earnestness, and cheerfulness are contagious." And then: "He has an inner orientation which draws him toward the sublime, and that will be his guardian angel."[2]

Hildebrand was deeply upset by the Nazi's enthusiasm for Wagner, which he thought was based on reasons antithetical to the spirit of the operas themselves. His position on Wagner is well-summarized in a passage from his memoirs describing the days leading up to his flight from Nazi Germany in March 1933:

> February 13 marked the fiftieth anniversary of Richard Wagner's death in 1883. I took this occasion to speak about Wagner's genius and his artistic work for the entire hour of my aesthetics class. I knew that real understanding for Wagner had declined since the First World War. The official Nazi admiration for Wagner rested on a complete misunderstanding of his work. For to approach the music of Wagner in search of overarching philosophical themes is to find the denunciation of power, the glorification of love and compassion, the rejection of the merely conventional, and the exaltation of the individual in contrast to all collectivism. There was therefore no basis for the Nazis to have such enthusiasm for Wagner.[3]

---

1. From *Adolf von Hildebrand und seine Welt. Briefe und Erinnerungen*, ed. Bernhard Sattler (München: Callwey Verlag, 1962), 512.

2. From *Adolf von Hildebrand*, 512.

3. From *My Battle Against Hitler*, by Dietrich von Hildebrand, trans. John Henry Crosby with John F. Crosby (New York: Random House/Image Books, 2016), 48.

The other major source of Hildebrandian commentary on composers is to be found in his *Aesthetics* vol. 2. While I have not included every mention of every composer, I have tried to feature sections that offer a larger appreciation of a particular composer or musical work, such as the section on Beethoven's *Fidelio*.

The 1962 published edition of *Mozart, Beethoven, Schubert* does not contain an author's foreword. I did find in the Hildebrand Archives at Franciscan University of Steubenville photocopies of two (and perhaps more) draft introductions by Hildebrand. It is unknown why the book was ultimately published without a foreword; perhaps Hildebrand or the publisher concluded that the essays could and should stand on their own. Given the unfinished and also more philosophical character of these introductions, I chose not to translate them for the present volume. The student or scholar wanting to enter deeply into Hildebrand's aesthetics will want to consider his discussion in these draft introductions of the respect in which his phenomenological approach informs his exploration of the composers and their works. The introductions develop at greater length Hildebrand's critique of the music critic influenced by historical relativism, which also appears in the opening pages of his essay on Mozart.

"Mozart" was first translated by me and published in English in the pages of the journal *Logos* (7:2, Spring 2004). My English translation of "Schubert" appeared in 2003 in the journal *Communio* (30.1, Fall 2003), on the occasion of the 175th anniversary of Franz Schubert's birth. I have significantly revised my translations of both essays for the present edition. My translation of "Beethoven" has never before been published in English; it appears for the first time in this volume. In addition to the original German book and the present English edition, an Italian edition of *Mozart, Beethoven, Schubert* is in preparation. The selections from "Wagner" were translated by me and first appeared in the *St. Austin Review* (July/August 2017).

In addition to Dietrich von Hildebrand's original footnotes, this volume also contains footnotes added by the translator to aid the reader with pertinent historical or other explanatory information. Any notes added by the translator are indicated by appearing in brackets.

I wish to thank several wonderful people whose contributions have greatly enriched this volume. First, I acknowledge in a very special way the late Madeleine F. Stebbins, who not only had a deep grasp of Hildebrand's thought and spirit (having been his student and friend), but who was unquestionably one of the most musically sensitive people I have ever known. Indeed, it is to Madeleine that I dedicate this English edition. I want to thank Mary Seifert for her sensitive comments on "Mozart" and "Schubert"; Susan Treacy who lent her musicological expertise; Alan Montgomery of the Oberlin Conservatory, and the late Nico Castel of the Metropolitan Opera who offered expert counsel on citing the operas of Mozart.

I am deeply grateful to Joachim Honeck, for assisting his father Manfred Honeck in preparing the beautiful foreword which graces this book, and also to Manfred himself for his friendship and support of the Hildebrand Project over many years. Finally, I offer grateful tribute to my dear father, John F. Crosby, my original collaborator in all things Hildebrandian, not just for reviewing and commenting on all of my drafts, but for gently admonishing me not to let the perfect become the enemy of the good.

John Henry Crosby
Steubenville, Ohio
May 7, 2024
200th Anniversary of the Premiere of Beethoven's 9th Symphony

MOZART, BEETHOVEN, SCHUBERT

Wolfgang Amadeus Mozart

ON HIS DEATHBED, CHOPIN SAID TO HIS FRIENDS, "Play something for me together and think of me as I listen to you." When his friend Franchomme said, "Yes, we will play your sonatas," Chopin exclaimed, "Oh no, not mine. Play for me the true music—that of Mozart."

Our hearts are filled with deep joy when we think of the words of love and admiration that have been spoken about Mozart—from Goethe to Hofmannsthal,[1] from Søren Kierkegaard to Theodor Haecker,[2] from Beethoven to Walter Braunfels.[3] Few great geniuses have been revered and loved as much as Wolfgang Amadeus Mozart. And yet it seems to me that not everything that has been said in praise of him has been said with true understanding. Along with wonderful expressions of the deepest insight, the praise is sometimes even painful because in truth it is not praise but a celebration of things that would not make Mozart greater if he possessed them, and which, thank God, he does not possess. This error is above all true of some contemporary "admirers," who are caught up in the fashionable trends of the day or are infected by historical

---

1. [Hugo von Hofmannsthal (1874–1929), prolific Austrian dramatist.]
2. [Theodor Haecker (1879–1945), German Catholic philosopher and theologian.]
3. [Walter Braunfels (1882–1954), German composer and Hildebrand's brother-in-law.]

relativism. Many music critics choose for themselves certain great artists whom they make into heroes of their "fashion" ideals and into whom they arbitrarily interpret, more or less consciously, things with which the artist has nothing to do. And so, in the age of "new functionalism,"[4] of neutralism and antipersonalism, in an age that scorns every "ethos" as "subjective" and romantic, one tries to brand Mozart as a kind of "ironist" and to pit him against the earnest and solemn Beethoven. There are a number of critics who praise Mozart at the expense of Wagner and even of Beethoven.

Instead of seeing that the individual differences between the great artistic geniuses in no way carry an antithetical but rather a complementary character—for example, between Michelangelo and Raphael, Titian and Giotto, Brueghel and da Vinci, or between Bach and Haydn, Handel and Schubert—these critics try to pit Mozart against Beethoven. Whoever does this can never understand the height, breadth, and depth of Mozart's spirit. Alexander Ulibishev is quite right when he says, "To love Mozart in all his masterworks means not to belong to any musical faction. It means to declare oneself for the beautiful and good in every category."[5]

There is only one real antithesis in the artistic realm, namely that between true art and bad pseudo-art; between powerful, inspired works of an inner necessity [*innere Notwendigkeit*] and tedious emptiness; between noble, authentic poetry and trivial kitsch. Whoever does not understand the ultimate greatness and depth of Beethoven's music, who approaches him with catchwords such as "subjective," "romantic," and "emotionally overwrought," who does not grasp the extraordinary objectivity and classicity of his symphonies and quartets or the unique artistic depth—full of mystery—of his late quartets, who has no inkling of the breathtaking inner necessity of the Ninth Symphony, who does not perceive the ultimate artistic word it contains, who is not deeply moved by the transfigured sacred depth of his *Missa solemnis*—to them also will remain hidden the mystery of Mozart's world, the soul of his art.

---

4. [See Hildebrand's "The New Functionalism in the Light of Christ," in *The New Tower of Babel* (Manchester: Sophia Institute Press, 1994), 91–111.]

5. [Alexander Ulibishev (1794–1858), Russian patron of the arts and Mozart biographer.]

Such a person would necessarily misunderstand Mozart, no matter how great a connoisseur of Mozart's works he was. Our hope is that every music critic misguided by fashionable trends and by the "Zeitgeist" might be affected by the spirit of Mozart as was the great Søren Kierkegaard who said, "You immortal one, to whom I owe everything, to whom I owe the loss of my reason—that my soul was stirred up and my innermost being was shaken—that I do not have to walk through life as one who is incapable of being deeply moved; you whom I thank that I do not die without having loved."

I do not wish to speak here about Mozart the man or about his life but rather about the genius of Mozart in his works. Many music historians expect to find in the life and person of the artist the key to his work. I believe, on the contrary, that we should let the work itself affect us without projecting something onto it. It is rather the other way around: the spirit of the work reveals to us the deepest level in the person of the artist, a spirit which he need not have radiated during his lifetime. Neither the person of the artist nor his life discloses to us the world and essence of his works but the works themselves, which, in the case of a great artist, usually far surpass what he realized as a human being. Apart from their own artistic content, the works reveal what was highest and deepest within the artist and for which he at least had a yearning. To actualize as a human being the spirit embodied by his work, Mozart would have had to be a saint—and that he was not.

When we look at his immense output, the inexhaustible richness of which seems like a miracle—and all this within a lifetime encompassing only thirty-five years—a world of sublime spirituality, unfathomable creative power, and inexhaustible poetry unfolds before us. In Mozart's work we find a unity of apparent antitheses, a *coincidentia oppositorum* (coincidence of opposites). Like that of no other, his art is angelic, of other-worldly sublimity, and yet like no one else's in being steeped in all that makes this world so ravishingly beautiful. His work is full of the enchantment of this world, full of the charm of life, full of humor; as hardly any other artist's work, it reflects the sweetness and delightful poetry of life and its many-sided situations. In his art reigns the exuberance of the most intense joy of life, an incomparable naturalness and immediacy, and a boldness and freedom of spiritual language [*geistigen Sprache*] over which, however, a transfigured splendor shines perpetually and the aura of another world hovers. Everything is suffused by an angelically transfigured air, everything is filled with a message from heaven.

Along with an extraordinary ability to give a definite spiritual shape and precision to his works as well as his brilliant ability to hit the mark, there is in Mozart's work a unique effortlessness. It is a special sign of the possession of a virtue that the good is done effortlessly; however painstaking the acquisition of a virtue, its possession is distinguished by effortlessness. This effortlessness of virtue presents itself in Mozart's art. Not the effortlessness of certain brilliant but lighter works of art, nor that of play, but the gift-like effortlessness that goes hand in hand with the greatest depth and precision of expression—an effortlessness that lies in the word "gratia," spanning everything from the highest meaning of "grace" [*Gnade*] to the "graceful" loveliness [*Grazie*] of outward manifestation.

In spite of all its inner necessity, Mozart's art is therefore permeated by a spirit of holy lavishness [*heiliger Verschwendung*] that we otherwise find only in nature. Richard Wagner has wonderfully characterized the essential character of Mozart: "A genius of light and love." Mozart's art is luminous. And not only is he a unique bard of love, but his music is itself filled with the genius of love; it is love transformed into music wherein dwells the radiance, the tenderness, the sweetness of true love. The way Mozart himself describes genius is deeply characteristic: "True genius without heart is an absurdity. For it is not high intellect alone, not imagination, not even both together that make genius. Love, love, love is the soul of genius."

Mozart is in a certain respect the most universal of the great musicians, for he created works of ultimate greatness in the most varied domains. Not only did he surpass everyone as a composer of operas, Mozart also created works of the highest beauty in his symphonies, his chamber music, and in the realm of church music.

Let us begin with Mozart as a composer of operas. The just-mentioned universality reveals itself in the fact that he—unlike other great operatic composers, such as Gluck, Wagner, or Verdi—created completely different basic types of possible combination of music and the stage. Mozart was not the only composer of operas of an extremely distinctive individuality; this is also true of Gluck, when we compare *Orfeo ed Euridice* with *Iphigénie en Tauride*, as well as for Wagner, when we think of the difference in the style between *Tristan und Isolde* and *Die Meistersinger*, and for Verdi, the creator of *Otello* and *Falstaff*. But in the operas of Mozart we find four quite different basic types of possible connection between music and dramatic action.

The first basic type we find in *The Abduction from the Seraglio*, the second in *The Marriage of Figaro* and *Don Giovanni*, the third in *Così fan tutte*, and the fourth in *The Magic Flute*.

In *The Abduction from the Seraglio* we have the type of German opera that reached its highest and most sublime expression in Beethoven's *Fidelio*. The relationship between the stage and the music here is characterized by the following elements: a dramatic plot with lofty moral content, in which the different characters retain a certain generality; the main characters filled with a moving human ethos, the supporting characters displaying an endearing humor. It is entirely fitting for the style of this type of opera that there is dialogue between the singing, not in a stylized recitative but spoken freely. The music, as it were, grows out of the spoken German. In contrast to Gluck, we find in *The Abduction from the Seraglio* a much more dynamic plot—not withdrawn into the world of antiquity and its strong style, let alone tied to a style determined by a particular epoch, like the operas of Handel.

The Abduction from the Seraglio is the earliest of Mozart's masterworks for the stage, the opera with a special personal touch, being written at the time of his engagement and marriage. In it there lives a happiness full of promise, a youthful note of hope. Carl Maria von Weber says of this opera, "This merry creation—glowing with the most exuberant youthful energy, virginally delicate in its sensibility—resonates with my personal artistic feeling and I have a special affection for it."[6] Here too, as in all of Mozart's operas, love stands in the foreground. The genius of love is

---

6. [Carl Maria von Weber (1786–1826), German Romantic composer known for his opera, *Der Freischütz*.]

uniquely manifested in the two magnificent arias of Belmonte in the first act. Especially beautiful is the purity and height of this love in the inexpressibly sweet music of Belmonte's second aria in the words, "Ist das ihr Lispeln? Es wird mir so bange. War das ihr Seufzen? Es glüht mir die Wange" ("Was that her whisper? I am so anxious. Was that her sighing? My cheeks are burning").[7] We are deeply moved by the extraordinary depth and dramatic power of the music in Constanze's great aria[8] in the second act and, above all, the great, sublime, tragic theme in the wonderful recitative in the last act, when Belmonte and Constanze believe everything to be lost.[9] The specifically dramatic genius of Mozart is also manifest in the aria sung by Osmin in the first act and also in the delightfully poetic "Romance" sung by Pedrillo,[10] which so perfectly shapes the situation; again, we see it in the sovereign freedom with which Mozart fashions the drama, perfect in every way, in the quartet in the second act,[11] particularly in the words of Constanze and Blondchen: "Wenn Männer verdächtig auf uns sehn, das ist nicht auszustehn" ("When men look at us suspiciously, it cannot be endured"[12]). Apart from its special style and its conception of the stage, *The Abduction from the Seraglio* as a whole, like all of Mozart's operas, bears the mark of a masterpiece. And yet in many places the music still rises above the framework of the drama; it hovers in heavenly height above the dramatic situation, which it thereby shapes in a masterful way.

In *The Marriage of Figaro* and in *Don Giovanni* we find a completely different type of drama, interpretation of the stage, and combination of word with music. Here we have Shakespearean drama in music: the full development of all characters as well as the various situations in their poetic power and intensity.

I know of no other comparison for *Figaro* than one of the comedies of Shakespeare, for example, *As You Like It*. One should not believe that it is

---

7. [Act I, Aria]
8. [Constanze sings two great arias in the second act. It is not clear which of these arias Hildebrand is referring to.—Trans.]
9. [Act III, Recitative and Duet.]
10. [Act III, Romance.]
11. [Act II, Quartet.]
12. [Ibid.]

Beaumarchais and da Ponte[13] that give *Figaro* its dramatic stamp. We need only compare Rossini's delightful *Barber of Seville* with Mozart's *Figaro* to see what a world separates these works; how Rossini expresses the Rococo world of Beaumarchais—graceful, witty, brilliant—whereas Mozart's opera, in its classical[14] humanity, the depth of its humor, and its sublime poetry, bears Shakespearean traits. To be sure, the music brings forth a world analogous to the world that Shakespeare expresses with words.

With this, the completely different conception of the stage in comparison to *The Abduction from the Seraglio* is already suggested: the much more ambitious dramatic aim, the new function entrusted to the music—a totally different type of drama. What characters, how dramatically developed to the utmost and how alive—a Figaro, a Susanna, the Count and the Countess, Bartolo, Basilio, the gardener Antonio, and that enchanting invention, original in the operatic literature and so quintessentially Mozartean: Cherubino! An incarnation of Mozart's youthful phase of being in love, Cherubino is a unique character and without counterpart in the whole of literature. But the same is true of every character. Mozart's music has made Figaro into an extremely attractive person, who is not only a highly talented servant and master of every situation, but also a human being filled with a noble moral ethos and a great, deep, and faithful love. How different he is from Rossini's Figaro! What poetry, what fragrance in Susanna and the Countess! Again we must recall Shakespeare, whose female characters, such as Viola, Rosalind, Perdita, Miranda, or Portia possess such an unspeakable charm and unique nobility, such a unity of inner moral beauty with the charm of their external being, which we encounter nowhere else in world literature. We find something analogous to these Shakespearean women in Mozart's *Figaro*. Mozart, too, succeeds in presenting female characters of indefinable

---

13. [The libretto for Mozart's *The Marriage of Figaro* was written by the Italian poet Lorenzo da Ponte (1749–1838). The plot of Figaro, however, was not original with da Ponte, who took it over from the second of three plays by French playwright Pierre-Augustin Caron de Beaumarchais (1732–99). The first of Beaumarchais's "trilogy" of "Figaro" plays was immortalized in Rossini's opera, *The Barber of Seville*.—Trans.]

14. [The word "classical" has a particular sense in Hildebrand's thought. See, for example, Hildebrand's discussion in "The Classical Spirit of the Liturgy" in *Liturgy and Personality* (Steubenville: Hildebrand Press, 2016), 111–22.—Trans.]

charm and fragrance, fully alive and as far removed from all naturalism as from classicist idealization—as real and natural as the loveliness of a splendid countryside.

The Shakespearean spirit is also revealed in the kind of humor found in *The Marriage of Figaro* and especially in *Don Giovanni*. Here it is not as with Osmin in *The Abduction from the Seraglio*, an essentially comic figure, but rather a much deeper humor as found, for example, in the scenes between Corin and Touchstone in *As You Like It*. Or again, we find this humor in the character of Basilio in the scene in which the Count discovers Cherubino[15]—where the music, as it were, is taken aback in amazement—in the appearance of the gardener Antonio,[16] and, above all, in the sextet at the words, "E questo è mio padre, che a te lo dirà ("And this is my father, he says so himself"[17]), expressing a classical humor that radiates a noble joy of life.

The Marriage of Figaro bears the special stamp of a masterpiece. What unparalleled unity of style from the first to the last note, what uninterrupted inspiration, every scene of the highest perfection! What a potent, unified artistic world the whole of *Figaro* is, filled with luminous power, with fragrance and poetry! What harmony between stage and music. There is hardly another work for the stage that is less problematic for performance, that can unfold its poetry completely within the framework of what the stage is capable of affording, in which the stage can effortlessly transport us into the world of the play.[18]

15. [Act I, Trio.]
16. [Act I, Finale.]
17. [Act III, Sextet.]
18. I cannot help pointing out the disastrous aberrations which many stage directors of Mozart performances fall into today. Instead of helping the viewer to be completely transported into the world of the music drama and to dwell imaginatively in the palace and park of Count Almaviva, to be drawn into the world of Mozart, instead of simply aiming to use the scenery in service of the artistic illusion—as one did in earlier times—these directors believe they should push themselves into the foreground with new ideas, and foolish ones at that, in which instead of the interior of a Rococo castle they erect an art nouveau room with an open sky above, which reminds us at every moment that we are sitting in a theater. This is a style of directing that forces us not to take the work seriously but rather to look at it as nothing more than a "performance" in a theater. And especially with *The Marriage of Figaro*, in which the work offers an ideal possibility for a poetic, artistic staging, the know-it-all attitude of modern directors is especially irksome. Even worse is the mindless speeding up of the tempos, the tendency to add as many staccatos as possible, to exaggerate the gesture of the

We find in *The Marriage of Figaro* an entirely new and extraordinary power of the music to heighten the dramatic situation, such as the two magnificent passages in the second act, "Deh, signor, nol contrastate, consolate i miei (I lor) desir" ("Please, lord, do not refuse (their wishes), grant my (their) wishes"[19]) and "Mente il ceffo, io già non mento" ("My ugly mug may be lying but I am not"[20]); or the theme when Susanna comes out surprisingly: "Signore! Cos'è quel stupore?" ("Your lordship! What is this amazement?"[21]) or when Antonio withdraws: "Parto sì, ma se torno a trovarti" ("I will go, but next time I see you"[22])—the progression of the music in the orchestra fashioning a fully dramatic situation. What radiance of deep and true joy suffuses everything, what a festive character in this indescribable work! In spite of its unity, strength, and breathtaking genius in the representation of a living world full of charm, the music rises again and again to a transfigured, otherworldly height, which lets us glimpse the splendor of a higher realm hovering above.

We encounter the same kind of Shakespearean drama in Mozart's greatest operatic masterpiece, *Don Giovanni*. Here, too, we find characters who are fully developed; we find the full depth of dramatic crafting, the rich and blossoming poetry. If we just compared *The Marriage of Figaro* to *As You Like It*, then *Don Giovanni* corresponds in its stature and dramatic form to a Shakespearean tragedy or to a play like *The Merchant of Venice*. Here Mozart unfolds before us the spirit of great and ultimate drama. The characters are more completed, more sharply developed: Leporello's warm-heartedness reminiscent in some of its traits of Sancho Panza, the sweet charm of Zerlina, the demonic Don Giovanni, Masetto, Donna Elvira, and the wonderful noble couple, Don Ottavio and Donna Anna.

---

music, to avoid all authentic, noble ethos and instead to add farcical, coarse effects. All this reveals a radical misunderstanding that seeks to reduce Mozart's art to the level of something artsy, soulless, brilliant but superficial, to treat him akin to Bernard Shaw rather than recognizing his ultimately Shakespearean depth and angelic nature. In contrast to these misinterpretations, I remember with gratitude the unique Mozart performances under Felix Mottl, Bruno Walter, and, as far as the musical direction is concerned, under Wilhelm Furtwängler in Salzburg.

19. [Act II, Finale.]
20. [Ibid.]
21. [Ibid.]
22. [Ibid.]

Don Giovanni has often been misunderstood, even by those who speak of it enthusiastically. The character of Don Giovanni is seen as the hero whom Mozart wants to exalt, Don Ottavio, on the contrary, as a feeble weakling. We have, however, only to immerse ourselves in the music with which Mozart characterizes Don Ottavio to grasp his unique nobility and moral strength. What a completely different note Mozart strikes in the music that embodies Don Giovanni! Yet this music, too, is extraordinarily beautiful and perfect, as, for example, the duet "Là ci darem la mano" ("There we will hold hands"[23]), the "Champagne" aria,[24] the wonderful passage "Vieni un poco in questo loco" ("Come here with me"[25]) the "Canzonetta,"[26] the aria "Metà di voi qua vadano" ("Some of you go this way"[27]) and many, many other passages.

Mozart's music always breathes an extraordinary purity, even when he is portraying the prototype of impurity. Yet the differences in the character of the music make it quite clear to anyone who has ears to hear who is more loveable in Mozart's intention, and nothing justifies the interpretation that Mozart wanted our sympathies to lie with Don Giovanni. True, Don Giovanni is not only presented as a villain, such as Pizarro in Beethoven's *Fidelio* or Iago in *Othello*, but characterized with many extra-moral excellences: he is lordly, fearless, of inexhaustible vitality, captivating, and endowed with the brilliance of irresistible success. Yet precisely this proves the dramatic greatness of Mozart—that he is capable of portraying the world in its reality and fullness, the broad stream of life, in which the wicked libertine, proud and lacking conscience, can be so full of seductive charm. Nevertheless, Don Giovanni is in no way worthy of love, neither in himself nor in Mozart's intention, but it is Don Ottavio and Donna Anna who deserve our love.

Like the greatest of all novels, Cervantes's *Don Quixote*, *Don Giovanni* in a certain way encompasses the whole length, breadth, and depth of human existence, indeed, of the universe—the world of noble and great

---

23. [Act I, Duet.]
24. [Act I, Aria.]
25. [Act II.]
26. [Act II.]
27. [Act II, Aria.]

love in its full moral depth, in its strength and splendor, embodied by Don Ottavio and Donna Anna, and the world of seductive vitality in Don Giovanni, which in spite of all its intoxicating fascination reveals an ultimate emptiness and tragic searching for joy where it is not to be found. Let us think of the almost leitmotif-like style that surrounds everything that has to do with Don Ottavio and Donna Anna. Beginning with the wonderful recitative of Donna Anna and Don Ottavio's reply, "Lascia, o cara, la rimembranza amara" ("Banish, my dear, this bitter memory"[28]), to the various arias of Donna Anna and Don Ottavio, to the theme in the "Trio of the Three Masks" in the first act when Don Ottavio and Donna Anna arrive at Don Giovanni's villa, and culminating in the musical highpoint of all arias, Donna Anna's "Non mi dir, bell'idol mio, che son io crudel con te" ("Do not tell me, my true love, that I am so cruel to you"[29]): at the appearance of Donna Anna and Don Ottavio, the music always bears the mark of special greatness, magnanimity, deep moral nobility, and true strength; always it emanates the breath of great, noble love against which Don Giovanni's courtly elegance stands forth clearly in all of its transitoriness and false splendor.

Even more fundamental is the immense antithesis between the Commendatore, representing the moral and religious world, and the success-obsessed evildoer, Don Giovanni. Can one find anything grander in music than the churchyard scene or the one in which the Commendatore comes to Don Giovanni—the ultimate, otherworldly seriousness in the musical rendering of the Commendatore, the breath of eternity, and the wicked insolence of the libertine, Don Giovanni? The Christian universe stands before us in all of its truth and greatness, and in wonderful contrast to this seriousness the deeply human figure of Leporello. Earthy and amiably this-worldly, Leporello embodies in all situations a simple, healthy commonsense analogous to that of Sancho Panza, who is, however, morally much nobler, or to that of the porter in *Macbeth*. We see this, for example, in the beginning, "Notte e giorno faticar" ("Night

---

28. [Act I, Recitative and Duet.]
29. [Act II, Recitative and Duet.]

and day I slave away"[30]), in the "Catalogue" aria,[31] and most of all in the incomparable music during the scene in the second act when Leporello is discovered to be disguised as Don Giovanni. Throughout the colorful and rich situations that convey the fullness of life, the figure of Leporello resonates like an organ—as representative of a primordial humanity and a deep, classical humor.

And how wonderful at the end, after Don Giovanni has been taken to hell after everything demonic has passed away, is the final scene of the opera, which is so down to earth and gladdeningly bright, that it captures the spirit of the entire work and so underscores the truth of it all. But even in this masterpiece of masterpieces—to which in the world of opera a place is due analogous to that of Beethoven's Ninth Symphony among symphonies—in which the inner necessity of every note shapes the drama and the dramatic world, be it "Metà di voi qua vadano" ("Some of you go this way"[32]) or "Zi, zi! Signore maschere! Zi, zi!" ("Psst! Psst! Masqueraders! Pst, pst!"[33]), the music in many places transcends the wonderful, rich poetic world of the drama of *Don Giovanni*, which at the same time is also shaped by the music, proclaiming the world of God through its redeemed and transfigured character.

In *Così fan tutte* we find a completely new, radically different conception of the stage and the possible connection between music and word. Here we do not have the Shakespearean drama of *The Marriage of Figaro* and *Don Giovanni*, but rather the drama of a Goldoni.[34] The characters are not fully developed but are rather general types—Don Alfonso, the cynic of the eighteenth century; Despina, the scheming servant like the character of Scapin in Molière's play. The remaining characters are not even this developed and are rather just carriers of the plot. The stage has

---

30. [Act I, Introduction.]
31. [Act I.]
32. [Act II, Aria.]
33. [Act I.]
34. Note well that the analogy to Goldoni concerns only the formal conception of the stage and drama. Goldoni manifests a morally noble tone in all of his works, which is almost entirely nonexistent in the libretto of *Così fan tutte*. Not the content of the libretto, but the formal method of dramatization is being compared here with Goldoni. [Carlo Goldoni (1707–93) was a prolific Italian playwright and librettist.]

the charm of entertainment; things flow lightly and with much variety. The music here does not have the task of fashioning fully dramatic characters as in *Figaro* and *Don Giovanni*; instead it cooperates, on the one hand, with the mood of the situation in the sense of Goldoni—the frequent use of two voices, the strong stylization, a different relation between word and song, a different role of gesture. On the other hand, the aforementioned soaring of the music above the plot into a sublime, transfigured world becomes much more conspicuous, precisely because the conception of the musical drama is not as intense. The quintet, "Addio" ("Farewell"[35]) and the following trio, "Soave sia il venta" ("May the wind blow gently"[36]) as well as the duet in the second act, "Secondate, aurette amiche, i miei desiri"("Friendly breezes, aid my desires"[37]), Fiordiligi's great aria, "Per pietà, ben mio, perdona all'error dun'alma amante" ("For pity's sake, my beloved, forgive the transgression of a loving soul"[38]) and the quartet at the end of the opera, especially at the words, "E nel tuo, nel mio bicchiero si sommerga ogni pensiero" ("And in your glass and mine may every care be drowned"[39]), all are of an unheard-of, sublime beauty, whose world far surpasses the Goldonian comedy without in any way bursting its framework.

This is true above all in the aria, "Un'aura amorosa del nostro tesoro" ("A loving breath from our sweethearts"[40]), which is one of the most beautiful of all Mozart's arias. I could not believe my eyes as I read in the introduction to the recording of a Glyndebourne performance that Mozart meant this "milksop" aria ironically. Apart from the fact that Ferrando sings this aria while he still believes in the faithfulness of his betrothed, Mozart is clearly speaking more generally here, uttering a primordial word from his soul, and expressing the genius of true and sublime love as only he can. It is so deeply characteristic that he, who created so many consummate masterpieces of drama, who could fulfill the genius

---

35. [Act I.]
36. [Act I, Trio.]
37. [Act II, Duet.]
38. [Act II, Rondo.]
39. [Act II, Finale.]
40. [Act I, Aria.]

of the theater so perfectly, by placing before us a powerful world unto itself, is also the one who with sovereign freedom expresses things that go far beyond the framework of the work. The angel of light, who dwells in Mozart, lifts up his voice at Mozart's command, unhindered and unconcerned about any style or framework. Herein we see again the spirit of divine lavishness of which we spoke at the beginning.

Thus, *Così fan tutte* joins the ranks of aforementioned operas as yet another masterpiece: entirely different in style, in the role of the stage, a completely different combination of music and word—a work consumate in every respect, seamless and borne by continuous inspiration, the delight of the enchanting *commedia dell'arte*, of precise diction, of wit, but at the same time beyond all this, the same genius of light and love as in all of his other works.

Unfortunately, *Così fan tutte* is often presented today as a pure satire, somewhat like Goethe's *Triumph der Empfindsamkeit*. The two girls, Fiordiligi and Dorabella, are presented with such exaggeration that they are made to be "précieuses ridicules,"[41] which is no way in the spirit of Mozartean opera. Certainly, they are intensely emotional in their expressions; their love is not very deep, but it is not simply affected. And yet the point is precisely that in spite of a sincere belief in their own love, they are weak and yield to cunning temptation. They are unsuspecting and naïve, not fancy puppets impressing us from the outset as caricatures. The singers should not involve the audience in making fun of themselves; otherwise it becomes a comedy routine or a clown act, and the Goldoni-style with its gracefulness and poetic charm is destroyed—to say nothing of the radical incompatibility of such portrayals with the unique music.

Most ridiculous of all is to think that Don Alfonso's opinions were shared by Mozart, to think that this pseudo-sage of the eighteenth century is not a character like Despina to be laughed at, a figure, among others, like Basilio in *The Marriage of Figaro*, but one with whom the author identified. It belongs precisely to this kind of comedy that neither in the

---

41. [A reference to Moliere's play, *Les Précieuses ridicules* (The Affected Ladies).—Trans.]

plot nor in the so-called moral of the story is there any declaration by the author. This is because the entire work is only a comedy, an amusing aspect of the world, not a great dramatic expanse comprising the whole universe in all of its great antitheses, as in *Don Giovanni*.

Also interesting for the difference in the dramatic conception of *Così fan tutte* is the predominance of wit—sometimes a bit of a caricature, such as Despina as doctor and notary—in place of the profound humor of *The Marriage of Figaro* and especially of *Don Giovanni* (Leporello comes to mind). Of course, Goldoni also does not provide comedy in the vein of Sancho Panza nor that of a classical Shakespearean humor, but rather an enchanting, ingeniously funny, slightly satirical representation of human weakness.

And now to the fourth, completely distinct conception of the combination of drama and music in *The Magic Flute*. It is not a drama like *The Marriage of Figaro* or *Don Giovanni*. We find here neither the Shakespearean fashioning of the characters, nor the general "types" in the Goldonian sense, not a stage world at all but a fairy play, whereby the characters are more the bearers of a particular ethos: Sarastro, the Queen of the Night, Pamina, Tamino, Papageno, Papagena, and so forth. Schikaneder's text,[42] with its sudden change—the Queen of the Night imperceptibly changing from good to evil—is not taken all too seriously; its function above all is to provide for an entirely new unfolding of Mozart's genius.

Mozart does not create an objective drama that is to be taken seriously in its own right, as in *The Abduction*, in *Figaro*, or in *Don Giovanni*. Neither does he present a highly stylized piece of *commedia dell'arte*, such as *Così fan tutte*. Rather, unconstrained by considerations of stage and plot, he creates the means for the full unfolding of worlds of sublime beauty, of the sweetness of being in love, of a solemn moral ethos, and of an entirely personal humor. The libretto enables a freedom of personal humor and a blossoming of naturalness, which is otherwise never to be found.

---

42. [Emanuel Schikaneder (1751–1812)—actor, singer, poet, and theater director—was the author of the libretto of *The Magic Flute*.]

The text here is rather an opportunity for creating a musical-poetical world like that of the Three Ladies at the beginning of the opera or that of "Drei Knäblein, jung, schön, hold und weise" ("Three boys, young, fair, lovely, and wise"[43]) at the end of the first part of the first act; or the wonderful coolness of the nightlike, crystalline coloratura arias of the Queen of the Night, the quintessentially classical world of being in love in Tamino's wonderful aria, "Dies Bildnis is bezaubernd schön" ("This portrait is enchantingly beautiful"[44]), and "Bei Männern, welche Liebe fühlen" ("With men who feel love"[45]); or the extraordinarily natural arias of Papageno, expressing a world of delightful nonsense, his "Hm, hm, hm, hm,"[46] or his encounter with Monostatos, "Hu! Das ist der Teufel sicherlich!" ("Hoo! That is the devil for sure!"[47]).

How sovereignly does Mozart surpass all rules, what blissful freedom, born of genius, do we find in "Das klinget so herrlich" ("That sounds so wonderful"[48]) or in "Pa- pa- pa- pa-."[49] What a contrast, what a juxtaposition between the sublime love of "Tamino mein!" ("Tamino mine! Oh what great joy!"[50]) and Papageno's "Ein Mädchen oder Weibchen" ("A sweetheart or a wife"[51]), or between "Bald prangt, den Morgen zu verkünden" ("Soon the shining sun … will proclaim the morning"[52]) of the Three Boys and the magnificent choruses of the Priests, "Pamina lebet noch!" ("Pamina still lives!"[53]) in the first act and "O Isis und Osiris, welche Wonne!" ("O Isis and Osiris, what bliss!"[54]) in the second. In *The Magic Flute* the above-mentioned effortlessness reaches its climax. With greatest ease and never pausing to take a breath, Mozart unceasingly pours out pure gold—the ultimate maturity of a transfigured depth.

43. [Act I.]
44. [Act I, Aria.]
45. [Act I, Duet.]
46. [Act I.]
47. [Act. I.]
48. [Act I.]
49. [Act II.]
50. [Act II.]
51. [Act II, Aria.]
52. [Act II.]
53. [Act I.]
54. [Act II, Chorus.]

The staging here is naturally much more problematic. The "delight of the stage" [*Wonne der Bühne*] of an opera like *Figaro* or *Don Giovanni* is unattainable, and yet the loose style of the fairytale facilitates entirely new things, both musically and even dramatically. There are new dimensions of the sung word, an effortless unfolding of overflowing beauty, and a grand symphonic character of the music, as in the fugue in the chorale-like music sung by the two armored men, all of which are dimensions that make *The Magic Flute* a high point *sui generis*. Yet I do not hesitate to repeat: Mozart's greatest, most perfect music drama, the last word of opera, is and remains his *Don Giovanni*.

This great fullness, this incredible multifacetedness, everything that we have mentioned so far concerns only one aspect of Mozart's musical creativity, namely the opera. Yet beyond this, Mozart's genius poured itself forth in his symphonies, his chamber music, and his sacred music. The limits of this essay do not permit me to go into these areas of his work in detail. The last symphonies—the "Haffner" and, above all, the "Prague," the symphonies in E-flat major and in G minor, and the "Jupiter" Symphony—confront us with a world of spiritual depth, masterful shaping, light, and noblest beauty. Everything is of inner necessity, extraordinary precision, and yet so lovely, coming to us as a gift. Whereas the great music dramatists—Gluck, Weber, Wagner, Verdi—have either hardly written a single symphony or else only ones that are far inferior to their operas, it is overwhelming to realize that Mozart, the greatest of music dramatists, is a master in his symphonies who even apart from his operas reveals himself to be a unique genius.

The same holds for his chamber music! The word that Mozart speaks here is of ultimate depth and genius. It is painful not to be able to mention all of the branches of his chamber music, not even to be able to single many of them out. A lifetime would not suffice to immerse oneself in each, to receive into one's soul the word that it speaks. I can mention only one pinnacle, one of the most sublime things ever to have proceeded from the human spirit, namely the Quintet in G Minor. A mysterious greatness, a necessity and inner form, a breathtaking, ultimate spirituality fills all of the movements and stirs us to our depths. In the theme of the third movement, the Adagio, we encounter a heavenly transfiguration before which all words fall silent.

We live in a time that is in danger of suspecting all beauty as saccharine, weak superficiality, a time that promotes a cult of ugliness, seeing greater depth in ugliness while finding harmony to be cheap and boring. What a message for our time is the chamber music of Mozart, what a refutation of this nonsensical, indeed, this evil enmity toward beauty! Think of the immense edifice of his piano concertos, of the world of inner joy and light, the inexhaustible river of grace-filled beauty to be found there or in the Fifth Violin Concerto and especially in the andante cantabile of the Fourth Violin Concerto. What a triumphant refutation of this modern perversion is Mozart's genius, which unfolds in all of its sweetness, depth, and angelic transfiguration in his chamber music.

In a time of the cult of originality at any cost, in which man no longer wants to recognize his creaturehood, in which he thinks that instead of using God-given ways and means of creating truly artistic values he must create an Esperanto of atonality, Mozart's chamber music, eternally young and inexhaustible, shows us what true originality is. Mozart himself writes in a letter, "How is it that my works take on the form or style of being Mozartean instead of being in the style of anyone else? It is just like the fact that my nose is so big and bent out that it is Mozartean and not like other people's noses! For I do not attribute it to individuality, and I would not even know how to describe my work more precisely; surely it's just natural that people who have a face also look differently one from another. And as this is true on the physical plane, so also on the spiritual. At least I know that I have given myself the one as little as the other."

To our age so lacking in reverence, Mozart's chamber music reveals the true spirit of reverence toward God and all high values, the conscious "yes" to our state as creatures. While today one all too frequently considers only tension and problems to be deep, all of Mozart's works, and especially his chamber music, resound with a radiant inner happiness and light. Although in many respects Mozart had a tragic life, one finds in the work of hardly any other genius such an affirmation of how beautiful creation fundamentally is. In spite of all the tragedy of the world, in spite of the very traits that justify us in speaking of this earth as a valley of tears—which Mozart knew as well as anyone—the words of the liturgy resound through his work: "*pleni sunt caeli et terra gloria tua*"—"heaven and earth are full of your glory." Yes, the world too is filled with God's glory; it too proclaims the eternal beauty of God; creation too abounds in mysterious beauty.

A festive radiance permeates Mozart's entire work. It shines, for example, in the Clarinet Quintet, the magnificent six quartets dedicated to Haydn, in his wonderful Clarinet Concerto, in his two extraordinary piano quartets, and in many divertimenti. In all of them, we encounter the deep recognition of the radiance of creation, of the festive character of all great things, and of the natural mysteries of this world. Mozart's work is the greatest antithesis to the radical disenchantment [*Ernüchterung*] of our times, to the depoeticization of the world, to the increasing blindness to the existence of spiritual realities, to the worldview that sees everything from below [*à* la *baisse*] and the reduction of reality to that which can be comprehended with the categories of natural science.

The true, deep humility that dwells in Mozart's work has been splendidly captured by Walter Braunfels in the following words:

> It is the human commitment to events, however they may come, sustained by a trust that all things come from God, which for Mozart strips reality of its problematic character and brings about a detachment, which at the same time is a true commitment to the reality of the present moment; for true detachment does not distance itself from reality, it only illuminates it with its special light from above. It is the humility which speaks out of Mozart's music in such a human way, lending it an aura of simplicity, which may seem almost facile to the superficial listener, but for one attentive to the essential, makes for what can stir most keenly—the lightest vessel with the deepest content. Only one who rests in God can transcend both sadness and serenity with such inner beatitude that these opposites of the human soul have a similar effect on us. Mozart's music is carried by an inner happiness that brings all emotions, both joyful and painful, into harmony. Humor and deep

seriousness seem to accompany one another in his art and in this life all the way to heaven's gates. It is humility before things as they are which makes Mozart's world so sublimely natural.

We would not do justice to the spirit of Mozart if we did not say a few words about his church music. Recently it was asserted by someone that Mozart's music is the typical representative of the spirit of Freemasonry manifesting no Catholic characteristics. Supposedly Mozart was a Catholic only out of tradition and for the sake of his father, while Freemasonry was his real inner conviction. This statement is again a typical example, on the one hand, of the above-mentioned arbitrary interpretation that presents an artist according to one's own wishes and prejudices. On the other hand, it is an example of the erroneous assumption that one comes to understand the spirit of a work of art through the biography of the artist. It is true that Mozart was a Freemason, for at the time Freemasonry was not yet seen as incompatible with the Catholic faith. This humanitarian fraternization was so much in fashion that Mozart and his father Leopold Mozart were Freemasons. But both were above all devout Catholics. Apart from the question of how Catholic Mozart was in his life, we must say: whoever does not sense the quintessentially Catholic character of Mozart's music when listening to it understands either nothing of the Catholic spirit or nothing of Mozart.

Mozart's only significant work in which one could find a relation to Freemasonry is *The Magic Flute*. Yet even here one could only say this of certain passages, such as Sarastro's arias, the choruses of the priests, and so on. We have only to compare "O Isis and Osiris" and "In diesen heil'gen Hallen" ("Within these sacred halls"[55]) with the Ave verum corpus or the Et incarnatus from the C Minor Mass to see the completely different and new manner with which Mozart treats the world of revelation and to understand that the redeemed, transfigured character which permeates his entire work derives its nourishment from religion, has its roots there, and takes on a specifically sacred tone in his church music.

If Bach's *St. Matthew Passion*, with its arias, choruses, and the role of

---

55. [Act II, Aria.]

the Evangelist, embodies the world of the Gospels in a unique way, so Mozart's sacred music—his Laudate Dominum, his Ave verum corpus, the Kyrie eleison, and above all the Et incarnatus from the C Minor Mass and the Recordare from the Requiem—is uniquely filled with the spirit of the One who says: "I am meek and humble of heart." There is also a Marian air that wafts in Mozart's sacred music; it breathes the spirit of glowing, heart-melting love; it is filled with the mystery of the Redemption.

If we find in Beethoven's *Missa solemnis* a spiritual kinship with Michelangelo's *Deposition from the Cross*, the work of his old age in the Duomo of Florence, or with his *Creation of Adam* in the Sistine Chapel, then the highpoints of Mozart's sacred music are in their ethos deeply related to two masterpieces of Raphael: the cartoons *Feed my Sheep* and the *Miraculous Catch of Fish* in the Victoria and Albert Museum in London—the same redeemed, sublime note, the same quality of mysterious holiness, the same quintessentially Catholic spirit.

This wonder, Wolfgang Amadeus Mozart, this most loveable, most irresistible of all great geniuses can be counted by Austria as one of her own. This land of music *par excellence*, which produced Haydn, Schubert, and Bruckner, is also the fruitful ground of Mozart's spirit and work. That Mozart's father came from Augsburg, with the result that Mozart is not as exclusively Austrian as Haydn, Schubert, or Bruckner, does not change anything. For it is a well-known fact that many of the greatest and most typical Austrians came from other countries, as, for example, Prince Eugene of Savoy.[56] Mozart's music is surely universal like all of the greatest masterpieces of art, surpassing every cultural framework in its mysterious greatness. At the same time, it is for anyone who has ears to hear a unique incarnation of the genius of Austria, of its supranational Catholic character, of its festive radiance, which fills Salzburg in such a special way, and of its modest and so-graceful countenance.

Hugo von Hofmannsthal says,

---

56. [Prince Eugene (1663–1736), a French nobleman in the service of the Austrian emperors, fought to drive the Turks out of Vienna in 1683.]

Mozart was here, and in these realms where the new and the old Europe touch, on this border between Roman, German, and Slavic culture, here his music arose, the German music, the European music, the true, eternal music of our time, the perfect culmination, natural as nature and innocent like it. Arisen from the depths of the most human of the German tribes, Mozart's music presented itself to Europe, beautiful and clear as antiquity, but a Christian, purified antiquity and more innocent than the first. Out of the depths of the people their deepest and purest being had turned to sound; tones of joy, emanating a holy, inspired spirit, light-hearted but not frivolous; a blessed feeling for life; the abysses sensed but without horror, the darkness still irradiated by heartfelt light.

We want to take our leave of Mozart with the words of Franz Schubert, whose name evokes another unique world of deepest poetry and unfathomable genius. In the mouth of Schubert, these words take on an especially moving note:

> This will remain for my whole life a clear, bright and beautiful day. As if from a distance, the magic sounds of Mozart are still quietly echoing within me.... Thus these beautiful imprints remain in our souls, which neither time nor circumstances can wipe away, acting in our lives for good. In the darknesses of this life, they show us a clear, bright, beautiful distance upon which we wait with confidence. Oh Mozart, immortal Mozart, how many, how infinitely many such consoling imprints of a luminous, better life have you impressed upon our souls!

Ludwig van Beethoven

IF ANYWHERE IN THE REALM OF ART we are reminded that God is the epitome of beauty, just as He is of goodness and truth, if anywhere we find revealed to us the ultimate, mysterious unity of the realm of beauty with that of the good and the true, if anywhere we can clearly perceive the ultimate and profound seriousness of beauty and the authentic mission of art, namely to be a voice that proclaims and leads to God, then we find it in the works of this artistic genius, in a certain sense the greatest of them all: Ludwig van Beethoven. For without wanting to place him above Mozart, Bach, Shakespeare, or Michelangelo, Beethoven, as we see in the ultimate artistic fashioning and consistent perfection of his works, embodies in virtually unsurpassed manner the genius of art as such. There are certainly artists who personally lived more deeply out of their faith and out of the supernatural, like Fra Angelico, Michelangelo, and Bruckner. There are also artists the content of whose works deal much more explicitly with the religious and which in a purely thematic way draw us to God and Revelation, like Dante, Bach, or Giotto. And there are artists whose works are suffused by a specifically unearthly, serene [*gelöstes*], and heavenly ethos, like Mozart and Raphael.

But in the case of Beethoven it is his very greatness and ultimacy as an artist, his penetration into the ultimate depths of which art is capable, that allows us to feel the breath of the Most High in his work, as we do in nature itself. It was once said with great profundity that if Bach could be compared to the most glorious architecture, then Beethoven could only be compared to nature.

In Beethoven's works we find a unique reflection of the cosmos and the objective realm of values in their classical hierarchy. No other artist is as comprehensive as he and so free from the limits of a single genre, from being trapped within a peripheral part of the cosmos, from all arbitrariness, from all personal hobby horses and eccentricities. Thus his art must be described as being specifically objective and classical.

It is finally time to show the complete misunderstanding that lies at the root of the cliché that Beethoven is the first great subjectivist who introduced the subjective element into the heretofore objective music of Bach and Mozart. The same applies to the related cliché about Beethoven as the first Romantic, the man of the nineteenth century in contrast to the representatives of the Classical period, Haydn and Mozart. Similarly, the image of Beethoven as the titan with the clenched fists is also an unfortunate legend. The alternatives "subjective" and "objective" as well as "Romantic" and "Classical" are entirely ambiguous. The term "Romantic," in fact, is used in three different senses without any distinction, indeed, without an awareness of the leap from one meaning to another.

In the first instance, the term "Romantic" has a purely historical meaning. It signifies the classification of an artist in relation to the epoch in which he was active. In this sense of the term we group as Romantics Schubert, Weber, Chopin, Schumann, Berlioz, Wagner, Brahms in contrast to the Classical figures Bach, Handel, Gluck, and Mozart, just as in literature we contrast the Romantics Eichendorff, Novalis, and E.T.A. Hoffmann with the Classical Schiller and Goethe. This classification in no way reflects any qualitative characteristics of the actual artistic content; it is purely historical and not aesthetic, for what Romantic composers in this sense of the term have in common are from an artistic point of view purely inessential outward appearances that do not contain any characteristics of the artistic world of each individual composer. They signify much less even than style does in architecture, which itself, of course, is just a language and not yet the artistic content. Keats and Eichendorff have just as little in common as do Chopin and Wagner.

"Romantic" can also have a completely different meaning when it refers to a particular quality of a work of art that characterizes the work independently of a purely historical classification. In this sense, Romantic refers to a looser form and a charming poetic quality in contrast to the monumental aspect of the Classical. It means to highlight a "colorful" element in contrast to an architectonic character. The art of Eichendorff is then Romantic, whereas Keats, though belonging to this same historical period, is thoroughly Classical and not Romantic. Or Weber's masterpiece *Der Freischütz* is Romantic, while *The Barber of Seville* is specifically un-Romantic.

Finally, "Romantic" can contain a negative value judgment, whether for the use of cheap effects, a subjectivistic note, a sentimental element in contrast to the truly objective character of true great art. Romanticism then refers to art whose form is not just looser but whose artistic content is blurred and cheapened in its quality. In this sense Grieg, or Schumann's *Traumerei* are perhaps Romantic, in contrast to Schubert or Weber who in this negative sense of the word are completely un-Romantic.

To call Beethoven a Romantic in any of the three senses of the term is, as one can easily see, quite impossible. Neither does he clearly belong historically into the nineteenth century, nor do any of the qualitative characteristics of the term "Romantic," which are applicable, say, to Weber, fit any of his music.

Wilhelm Furtwängler says in his essay on Beethoven,[1]

> What strikes one above all about Beethoven, and manifests itself to a greater extent in his music than in that of others, is what I would call

---

1. [Hildebrand quotes several times from the essay by German conductor Wilhelm Furtwängler (1886–1954), "Die Weltgültigkeit Beethovens," in *Ton und Wort* (Wiesbaden: F.A. Brockhaus, 1954). An English translation of this essay, "The Universality of Beethoven," appears in the book, *Furtwängler on Music*, Ronald Taylor ed and trans (Aldershot: Scolar Press, 1991). Quotations from the German essay are translated by me.—Trans.]

the "inner law." More than any other composer he strives after what is naturally fitting, for what is definitive—hence the extraordinary clarity that distinguishes his music. The simplicity that dominates his work is not that of a naïve or a primitive artist.... And yet no music has ever been written that approaches the listener so directly, so openly—so nakedly, so to speak.[2]

Even less do we find in Beethoven's work anything Romantic in the sense of an artistic disvalue.

Furtwängler continues,

And this special form of clarity entails renouncing all those methods—which are to be found in art just as they are in life—for setting what one has to say in as favourable a light as possible, using formulations and emphases that make it appear more important and more profound than it actually is.[3]

Also ambiguous are the terms "objective" and "subjective." Objectivity is often identified with neutrality. This is a particular error of our time which finds its typical expression in the ideal of the so-called "*neue Sachlichkeit*," or "new functionalism."[4] Within this framework, all that is affective or personal, every ethos, radiance, or ecstasy is subjective and lacking objectivity. Ultimately, this ideal is part of the general antipersonalism that is embodied in the most terrifying way in the totalitarian idols.

The identification of neutrality and objectivity is a disastrous error. The measure of objectivity is inner fittingness, correspondence with the logos of being, and the adequate response to the world of values. The person as such is in no way unobjective; affective value responses of real joy, authentic sorrow, and true love are the epitome of objectivity in the true sense of this term.

---

2. ["The Universality of Beethoven," 38. Translation revised.]
3. [Ibid. Translation revised.]
4. [Hildebrand devotes an entire essay to this theme: "The New Functionalism in the Light of Christ," in *The New Tower of Babel* (Manchester: Sophia Institute Press, 1994), 91–111.—Trans.]

We only find subjectivity among persons in a negative sense in things like an inappropriate response, in error, prejudice, sentimentality, self-indulgent sorrow, pseudo-love. Precisely in valid personal acts, like true love, true sorrow, or true joy, do we find the specific antithesis to the subjective in this sense.

We can speak in various senses of "subjective" as a flaw in art. In the first place it can refer to works in which the actual objectification [*Objektivierung*] in the sense of being fully formed is lacking, where the transformation into the world of art is not wholly successful, where the projection by which the work of art receives its independent existence and becomes the bearer of artistic contents is missing. A work may be filled with a lofty intention and a noble ethos, but lacking the transformation into the objective language of art. Many of Schiller's works, for example, are typical examples of subjective art in this sense.

It is not difficult to see that all this is totally antithetical to the spirit of Beethoven. Surely there is no other artist in whom we find such complete artistic fulfillment, such a conscious striving for specifically artistic worlds, such intentional realization of these worlds to the very last detail. Whether we look to his quartets, piano concertos, or symphonies, to *Fidelio* or the *Missa solemnis*, always we encounter the realm of art in the purest expression of its own artistic language. Never in Beethoven do we find an ethical intent serving as a surrogate for the work of art or simply placed untransposed alongside the work; everything bears the mark of ultimate, goal-conscious perfection, such that Beethoven in this sense must be described as the most objective of composers.

There is yet another sense of subjectivity in art, namely when one means the quality of the ethos that fills a work. There is a kind of art in which a spirit of taking oneself seriously is dominant, a subjectivistic reveling in one's feelings, a capricious giving into one's moods, art which is not dictated by the objective logos but by the artist's desire to display himself. We find here an ethos that lapses easily into sentimentality and which is suffused by self-indulgence and arbitrariness.

The art of Beethoven, by contrast, is an unsurpassed expression of the objective logos. The ethos suffusing it is through and through that of a reverent and profoundly felt value-response, of a surrender to the world of values and to God. Nothing could be further removed from a spirit of self-indulgence and taking oneself too seriously.

Furtwängler says: "Beethoven never wants to appear 'profound'; he does not want to 'appear' at all; he simply is—and herein we see his true depth and his real innocence."[5] What a classical ethos of self-gift do we find in the portrayal of love in *Fidelio* or in the Lied *An die ferne Geliebte*.

The objectivity and classicity[6] of Beethoven's art is also revealed by the singular perfection attained by "form" in his music. We have here a form completely filled from within and free from all conventionalism, a form which in every moment represents a new invention and precisely for this reason contains a perfect inner logic and lacks all arbitrariness. Even in this ultimate interpenetration of form and artistic ethos we see to what a high degree Beethoven's art is an expression of the objective logos. To speak of a rending or bursting of form in an artistic sense is completely inapplicable to Beethoven. Whoever says this falsely equates the quality of a certain neutral ethos with the presence of artistic form.

Beethoven is perhaps the most conscious artist [*bewußteste Künstler*] there has been, conscious in the sense of working in an intentional manner. It is widely known how Beethoven worked on his compositions, how inspiration would break into the process of conscious work, unlike, say, Mozart where we find rather the unconscious reception of a gift. Beethoven would work for a long time on a single work until he had realized that which his genius had provided to him. Nothing would be more shortsighted than to see this conscious producing as antithetical to brilliant inspiration. This is no ordinary, purposeful work that goes in search of inspired material that it can use and develop; quite the contrary, in Beethoven the process of conscious working is itself thoroughly inspired.

If one compares the first sketches of the "Eroica" with the final work, one can clearly see what an artistic ascent takes place as Beetho-

---

5. ["Die Weltgültigkeit Beethovens," 187.]

ven worked through his material, how the decisive ideas arrived only in the process of development. This is why Beethoven's works lose nothing of the immediacy and gift-character of the initial inspiration, despite representing the ultimate in artistic fashioning and consummate development. Indeed, the marvelous draft, the bold, sweeping momentum of certain splendid and brilliant sketches are fully present in Beethoven's works alongside the ultimate in expressive perfection and the absence of anything unfinished [*Skizzenhaft*]—a unique combination of excellences which are usually mutually exclusive.

The depth and freedom of certain sketches rests on the fact that, with a single musical line, at once bold, great, and simple, so much is encompassed, profoundly uttered, and delicately intimated. Beethoven possesses this depth and freedom in music fashioned to the minutest detail and differentiated to the highest degree. Even the character of hushed mystery that marks certain sketches, a quality easily lost in the course of the detailed activity by which a work is brought to full reality, is completely preserved in Beethoven's finished work. We have only to think of the "Eroica", of the beginning of the second act of *Fidelio*, or of the first movement of the Quartet opus 132.

This is why Beethoven—the very incarnation of form, in whose music, as Furtwängler so beautifully says, the "inner law"[7] reigns beyond compare—is also the greatest antithesis to all that is academic and conventional. Indeed, we must go further. Often the qualities of being fully formed, of clarity and precision, of leaving nothing unsaid, stand in contrast to mystery and to the "infinite," to that which can only be indicated by intimation. These two elements interpenetrate in Beethoven. If we think of the first movement of the Ninth Symphony, we find that everything is uttered with tremendous inner necessity and fashioned with ultimate consciousness. Nevertheless, no other work communicates to us more the infinite depth behind what is spoken, no other in which clear and sharply contoured form evokes less a "feeling" of finitude. Both elements interpenetrate to such a degree that precisely what is mysterious

---

7. ["The Universality of Beethoven," 38.]

and ineffable is given with extraordinary clarity and that what is fully expressed not only leaves ajar the door to the ineffable but even opens it. In Beethoven's work there dwells something of the spirit that allows St. Augustine to say in his *Confessions*:

> You are my God, my Life, my holy Delight, but is this enough to say of you? Can any man say enough when he speaks of you? Yet woe betide those who are silent about you! For even those who are most gifted with speech cannot find words to describe you.

The same Beethoven, who speaks so unerringly, who utters everything with such consciousness and inner necessity, nevertheless possesses the amazing discretion of "leaving open" [*Offenlassen*] or, as we could also say, he has no pretension of having left nothing unsaid; he is utterly opposed to any rationalism and to any thin academic clarity.

In every art form, one of the essential elements of true greatness is inner necessity. Masterworks are all characterized by the fact that nothing is accidental in them, that they are convincing at every stage, and that one has the sense: yes, this is how it must be and not otherwise. This necessity reaches a unique highpoint in Beethoven. Nothing is simply approximate, nothing could be otherwise, and this inspiring and convincing necessity grows with Beethoven's own inner development and in the Ninth Symphony reaches a pinnacle that is unsurpassed in the entire sphere of art, whether in the visual arts, music, or literature. This necessity is deeply bound up with the consciousness and fully fashioned character of Beethoven's works.

Beethoven was also especially conscious in the sense that he strove for the world of the specifically artistic in its ultimate seriousness and depth. He did not realize the loftiest artistic worlds more or less unawares by attending to ethical problems or other matters of content, or even to technical problems, but by consciously aiming at what constitutes the ultimate meaning and mission of art. This is not an ex post facto or purely theoretical relation to the artistic, which would represent a sort of surrogate for the original act of creation, as for example in Lessing and other artists in Romanticism or German Idealism, but rather one where the artist in his totality, even in his conscious being, is seized by an artistic genius, where he is filled with such an abundance of creative power, where he becomes such an incarnation of the world of art in his very person, that it leads him to an ultimate, conscious understanding of the secrets hidden within the realm of beauty. Only the most conscious artist in this sense could write works like the late quartets. Only such an artist could penetrate into these ultimate artistic depths, into the undiscovered possibilities of ultimate seriousness that are here to be found and which allow the listener, even absent any explicitly religious themes, to feel the closeness of the Almighty.

In Beethoven, the theme emerges in a special way alongside the melody. This form of musical inspiration takes on an ever greater importance in late Beethoven, where a short, compact musical line contains an inexhaustible fullness of beauty, artistic content, and poetic worlds, such that whenever such a theme sounds anew, it always exerts the same mysterious effect. It can and must be repeated much more frequently than the actual melody itself. A theme also has a more potent spiritual quality in relation to a melody, somewhat similar to the bare musical note in relation to a melody. We have only to consider the opening theme of the Ninth Symphony, the themes in the scherzo of the same work, or those in the late quartets. With this sheer spiritual quality we touch on a special characteristic of the late Beethoven. In the late quarters from opus 127 to 135 we find a mysterious spiritual ethos [*Geistigkeit*], a breaking through into a pure primordial artistic substance, and at once an inmost, solitary word of ultimate transfiguration and sublimity.

Unique in Beethoven is the sheer diversity that he can draw out of a single melody or theme. We find this, say, in the allegro theme in the last movement of the Quartet opus 59, no 1, whose cheerful liveliness follows on the magnificent and tragic adagio. At the end of the second movement, this theme surprises us by returning slowly and solemnly, with profundity of feeling and as if from a distance, like a magnificent light on the horizon. How extraordinarily this music is fashioned! How remarkably Beethoven continues the development of a thematic idea! We find the same in innumerable passages in Beethoven, such as in the marchlike treatment of the theme "Freude, schöner Götterfunken" ("Joy, fair divine spark") in the last movement of the Ninth Symphony.

Finally, the ethos that pervades Beethoven's art is conscious. This consciousness in Beethoven's ethos gives his works a seriousness, a sublimity and depth, that we find analogously only in Michelangelo. It is an intensification in the direction of a reverent, deeply felt self-giving; we could as well say: in the direction of the fundamentally theocentric orientation of Beethoven's world, which very sharply distinguishes him from any self-indulgent nostalgia as it is found in Romanticism in the negative sense. Not only does this consciousness not deprive his works of a certain chasteness characteristic of naïvete in a positive sense, but it unites a unique spirituality, awakedness, and transfigured quality with a simplicity and solitary greatness; it leads to an immediacy and simplicity that we encounter only in nature with its direct proclamation of God's glory. Furtwängler says: "For all of the power that sweeps through this music, a holy sobriety, as it were, compels it into the law of the organic. It is explosive, indeed ecstatic to the very limits of human experience—and nevertheless not in the slightest overwrought."[8] Precisely this consciousness is a special attribute of Beethoven's objectivity.

The reverent, value-responding attitude which pervades Beethoven's works—and which represents the absolute antithesis to all that is arbitrary, unserious, aestheticist, or frivolous in any further sense—excludes from the outset the titanic, cramped, tragic gesture that has been imputed to Beethoven. The solitary tragedy of Beethoven the man, who had to contend with a difficult fate, has been interpreted, contrary to his own assurance in the Heiligenstadt Testament, not just as a core personal characteristic but has also been projected onto his work. Those who wanted to find in the ethos of his works a rebellious, titanic element soon marked him as the titan bursting the old, rigid form; this in turn led to seeing him as the metaphysical revolutionary whose spirit exudes a promethean rejection of God and the objective hierarchy of values. Nothing could be more erroneous. The person whose only relationship to

---

8. ["The Universality of Beethoven," 39, translation revised.]

art comes from associating it with a particular social image of the artist or even just with the atmosphere of the time in which the artist lived may believe wrongly that they have found such things in Beethoven; they are unable to grasp what his works themselves convey. In truth, no other ethos is more affirmative than Beethoven's, none more commensurate to the world of values; if there is any protest in his music, it is only to the extent that it stands at odds with all that is base, coarse, mediocre, purely conventional, and petty. Indeed, we encounter in Beethoven's art the objective world of values in their classical structure; an art in which all genuine goods are intimately understood and precisely for this reason bears unswerving and ultimate witness to the "Father of Lights."

In Beethoven's art we encounter an awesome power [*Kraft*], which we find otherwise only in Michelangelo. His art is immense, without ever being coarse or of elemental, uncontrolled power, and without ever rupturing the form. We need only think of the tremendous succinctness, the breathtaking force of the Ninth Symphony, the joy to the point of bursting in the scherzo of the Ninth, which is simultaneously a highpoint of tautest form. One thinks of the force of the finale of the Fifth Symphony or the first movement of the "Eroica." This forcefulness is surely the origin of the legend of the titan with the clenched fist. One falsely thinks that awesome power can only be found in protest, in the rejection of divinely intended order, in a revolutionary gesture, in disharmony. This is a great error. One fails to recognize that the greatest power lies in order, that the divine power manifests itself in the laws of nature, that creation exhibits proportion and order and not chaos.

Beethoven's power is not that of the titan with the clenched fist, nor is the tragic dimension in many of his works, such as the second movement of the "Eroica," the adagio of the "Harp" Quartet, the Cavatina, and much else that of the rebellious titan or the metaphysical pessimist. In Beethoven, we have the true tragedy of the "*vallis lacrimarum*" ("valley of tears"), behind which stands the victorious joy which has the last word. This victorious joy dwells in Beethoven in a unique way, sorrow and joy shining forth in their true classical relationship. Beethoven penetrates the deepest mysteries of suffering, but he is also unsurpassed in expressing the full range of joy and happiness, from the high spirits in the final movements of the Fifth and Sixth Quartets opus 18, the radiant joy of the final movements of the Fourth and Fifth Piano Concertos, the bursting, intense joy in the final movement of the Quartet opus 59, no 2, the radiant, boundless happiness in the Pastoral Symphony, the first and last movement of the Fourth, Seventh, and Eight Symphonies, to the victorious ecstasy of joy in the final movement of the Ninth and the deeply felt beatitude in the Benedictus of the *Missa solemnis*.

Indeed, think of the final movement of the quartet opus 130. This movement is the last thing Beethoven composed as a very sick man facing death. Nothing is more moving than the serene, radiant joyfulness of this movement, the last word, which follows upon the incomparable, sublime Cavatina.

What an abundance of voices of nature [*Naturwelten*] do we find in his symphonies, what a free and unfettered lightheartedness in the scherzi, which represent the greatest antithesis to any tragic outlook. The more we really attempt to enter into his symphonies, the more clearly we will perceive the victorious affirmation, the voice speaking out the objective hierarchy of values, out of an ultimately harmonious cosmos. Do we not find reflected everywhere in Beethoven, say in the Eighth Symphony, a total and unconstrained "going with" [*Mitgehen*] the objective rhythm of the world of values? If we call Beethoven titanic, tense, and bombastically tragic, then we can just as well call nature, in its simple grandeur and humble proclamation of God, titanic and emotionally overwrought. Where else can we find a less problematic glorification of love than in *Fidelio*, in the singularly magnificent figure of Leonore? Why is Beethoven roused not by some bizarre problem, by something antagonistic, by some untamed, destructive passion but instead inspired to depict the noblest spousal love and fidelity? Who can hear the Prisoners' Chorus in *Fidelio*, or the ensemble at the moment where Leonore frees Florestan from his chains, without perceiving this ethos, filled with deeply felt reverence and steeped in an ultimate spirit of value-response, without understanding that all titanic discord finds its utter antithesis here?

We said in our essay about Mozart that he is the most universal composer because he achieved the greatest heights in all domains, whether in opera, symphony, chamber music, or sacred music. But we can describe Beethoven as the most universal or comprehensive musician in an entirely different sense. Despite the amazing diversity of Mozart's musical colors and musical conception, he remains in a certain sense always the same. By contrast, Beethoven enters so deeply into the distinctive character of the sonata, the symphony, the quartet, the violin sonata, the piano concerto, that he draws out completely different qualities according to each particular musical form. Despite all the particular differences among the individual sonatas, symphonies, and quartets, we can speak of a Beethoven of the sonatas, a Beethoven of the symphonies, a Beethoven of the quartets. He takes a given musical form much more seriously than any other composer, realizing its particular meaning and special character to such a high degree that with him, and only with him, do we have the feeling of hearing *the* sonata itself, *the* symphony, *the* quartet. The G-Minor symphony of Mozart may be as beautiful as the Fourth or Fifth Symphony of Beethoven, but the Beethovian symphonies are the symphonies *par excellence*, the fulfillment of the essence of the symphony, the archetype of the symphony. The same is true for his piano sonatas, and all the more so for his quartets.

This holds in a special way for the *Missa solemnis*. Here we encounter a whole new side of Beethoven, which above all has the character not just of *a* mass but of *the* mass itself. The masses of Mozart bloom quite naturally in the religious setting of the church, but in the case of the *Missa solemnis* we find the intention to set the mass as such in an artistically valid way, and not just the intention but the full realization. When we consider this ultimate realization of each of the various musical forms, we can see that Beethoven in this sense must be described as the most universal of all composers.

Beethoven's work as a whole represents an inexhaustible world of sublimest beauty and greatness. It is as if Beethoven created by drawing on the very core of musical possibilities, everywhere uttering the decisive, valid word. What ultimate beauty, what significant, breathtaking depth are revealed in his quartets, what world-encompassing greatness in his symphonies! In his piano concertos, the piano displays all its brilliance, its dazzling power in performance, a spirit of bold exultation. In the Violin Concerto, the sublimity and hovering transfigured quality of this soul among the instruments comes to full expression. What a world of musical flowering, what a treasury of beauty in his piano sonatas, what a new quality in the magnificent violin and piano sonatas, and in the piano trios! Certainly, Beethoven's Lieder are not of the same level as his other works, insofar as they are not the fulfillment of the very idea of the Lied, namely, the most perfect union of poetry and music, as we find it in Schubert. Nevertheless, *An die ferne Geliebte* is the most beautiful Lied that has ever been written. And the Scottish Songs, what a unique creation, how marvelously the special charm of the folk song is captured in this chamber music!

Of course, *Fidelio* is not *the* opera as all of Beethoven's symphonies are *the* symphonies, his chamber music *the* chamber music, the *Missa solemnis*, *the* mass.

Many dimensions of opera—such as the dramatic fashioning [*Durchgestaltung*] of all the characters, even minor ones; the fulfillment of all that the stage and the theater in the highest sense of the term have to offer; the humor and comedy that find their highest embodiment in Mozart—are not developed in *Fidelio*. And yet *Fidelio* is an ultimate pinnacle in opera; it possesses a unique dramatic quality found only in it; and it opens horizons of human depth which Mozart did not even aspire to give. We have only to think of the grand scene of the liberation of the prisoners in the second act.

The immense drama of the trumpet call, which breaks auspiciously into a moment of utmost tension as a saving light, a highpoint in the dramatic action, is taken up in the most extraordinary way by the inner drama of the duet, "O namenlose Freude" ("Oh inexpressible joy!").[9] What Beethoven offers in this duet is absolutely remarkable. What a stroke of genius that, without concern for the plot—the Minister's arrival and Pizzaro's ascent from the dungeon—Beethoven asserts the absolute priority of the great love between Fidelio and Florestan, their reunion,

9. [Act II, Duet]

the fulfillment of their yearning at long last. In this moment the world falls away, everything recedes, and the interior space of love itself forms a dramatic conclusion. What an extraordinary dramatic conception we find in this ecstatic highpoint, in the "finality" of finding each other again, the knowledge that "all now is well."

And what an expression of beatitude, of the most moving and intense love, of devout gratitude to God, all extraordinary elements for a finale! The presentation of ultimate fulfillment as this music fades away is simply beyond description. This is one of those moments, like the Prisoners' Chorus and "O Gott, welch ein Augenblick," ("Oh God, what a moment is this"),[10] that ensures *Fidelio* a completely unique place among operas for its seriousness and depth. We find nothing like this in Mozart, despite his unique genius as a dramatist and his Shakespearean fashioning of every character. But Beethoven's power and greatness in conveying a dramatic situation, which moves us to the core and which, as in *Fidelio*, is filled with ultimate human seriousness, this Mozart simply does not possess.

Here we come to a noteworthy difference between Mozart and Beethoven. Beethoven identifies himself personally with his work to a completely different degree from Mozart. Even though Beethoven is unsurpassed for his objectivity and though he presents worlds that are specifically objective, his entire work, and especially the Ninth Symphony, the *Missa solemnis*, and *Fidelio*, contains a confessional[11] [*Bekenntnis*] dimension, which is not the case in Mozart's works. Both of them also have a different relationship to art, to the public, and to success. For Beethoven art is much more immediately a kind of liturgy [*Gottesdienst*], something extraordinarily earnest, much as it was for Michelangelo. It would be unthinkable that he would say of an aria in *Fidelio*, "this will elicit a rousing bravo and need to be repeated many times," as Mozart could say. All that Mozart touched turned to gold; he could have the most wonderful inspirations even in a divertimento, pearls Beethoven would never scatter in incidental music.

10. [Act II, Finale]
11. ["Confessional" here has the sense of "confessor," as in to bear witness, not of "confessing" one's sins.—Trans]

It is deeply characteristic of Beethoven that he could never understand how Mozart could choose libretti like "Così fan tutte" or "Figaro." The Shakespearean objectification of the stage, a seriousness that is entirely rooted in the poetry and in which the author does not confess personally, was foreign to Beethoven. But this confessional element gives *Fidelio* a uniquely moving depth and also a greatness of a purely artistic kind. This confessing, which is sometimes wrongly interpreted as being "subjective," makes Beethoven unbearable for a time that seeks to evade all depth.

Another fundamental characteristic of Beethoven's music, one closely tied to this "confessional character," is the significance [*Bedeutsamkeit*] that breathes in all his works. Beethoven never merely "makes music"; he is never the captive of a cheap musical logic; every word is fully valid, consciously placed, significant, a full realization, a precise, unique and definitive content. On the whole this significance increases with Beethoven's advancing development; it is stronger in the middle Beethoven than in the early. What an extraordinarily significant word of ultimate validity is spoken in the Violin Concerto, the First Razumovsky Quartet, in the Fourth and Fifth Piano Concertos, in the *Leonore* Overture, in the "Eroica" and in the Seventh Symphony.

This character of significance takes on an entirely new note in the late quartets and in the *Missa solemnis*. But then in the Ninth Symphony we experience something totally unique, as if Beethoven were crying out to us: "Listen carefully, now I will say everything." This significance does not mean that Beethoven is always "tense." By no means! Beethoven is unsurpassed in conveying the objective worlds of nature [*Naturwelten*] in their vast serenity. No one conveys the primordial poetry of the pastoral as Beethoven does in the Piano Sonata opus 26, in many symphonies, not only in the *Pastoral* Symphony, but also, for instance, in the Fourth Symphony, in the first movement of the Seventh, and in the second movement of the Quartet opus 132 where the strings attain an almost flute-like character.

Beethoven is again unique in that there is no other artist who has his all-embracing balance, itself a *coincidentia oppositorum* (coincidence of opposites).

In his art, all the elements of the cosmos of values come to expression. No *one* element is ever exclusively predominant, whether the tragic or radiantly joyful, the tender, the powerful, the dramatic or the epic, tension and tranquility, sweetness and bitterness; rather, *all* of them come to expression and in their classical hierarchy, indeed, in absolute balance. In this Beethoven distinguishes himself completely from Michelangelo, with whom he otherwise has such deep affinity. In Michaelangelo, certain basic categories of the world of values are predominant, such as the tragic, the magnificent, the powerful, a depth of concentration, the ecstatic. He does not possess this totality of Beethoven who encompasses in equal measure sublimity and high-spiritedness, mystery and simple clarity, poetic loveliness, power, profound tragedy, joy in all its levels, the dramatic and the contemplative, ecstasy and complete tranquility, light and dark. As Furtwängler rightly says,

> Nowhere in all of European music is there another composer in whom the various elements of the songful and the purely structural, the tender and the firm, which only in their unity comprise a natural, living organism, have formed such a natural synthesis; no other composer in whose music the skin, flesh, and bone of a living body—to speak of what we ourselves are made—are so organically and naturally combined.[12]

One quality which Beethoven possesses to a special degree is the heroically victorious [*heroisch Sieghafte*]. Neither Bach nor Mozart, Haydn nor Schubert embody this element in their works like Beethoven. Nor does Handel, with his unique festive spirit and grand Baroque gesture, have the specifically heroic, victorious quality which we encounter in the Egmont Overture or in the Third, Fifth, and Ninth Symphonies.

Closely tied to this is the "boldness" [*Kühnheit*] in Beethoven, a boldness which can analogously be found only in Wagner, although in an entirely different form. Neither Bach or Handel, nor Mozart, Haydn, or Gluck have this specific quality of boldness.

Beethoven possesses a unique freedom. In spite of the tremendous

---

12. "Die Weltgültigkeit Beethovens," 185–86.

form, despite the "inner law," the ultimate inner necessity and binding logic, we find a sovereign freedom in his works. At the end of the second movement of the Violin Concerto or in the adagio of the String Quartet opus 127 or in the adagio of the Ninth Symphony or the Benedictus of the *Missa solemnis*, we find a contemplative lingering, a free, hovering way of drawing out of the musical line, a blissful, redeemed freedom. It is like the completely unconstrained unfolding of the most precious, deepest sublimity. This is different from the sacred progression in Bach's Air, C Major organ toccata, or in the second movement of the Double Concerto; again different from the angelically transfigured voice of Mozart. It is impossible to express this special contemplative note in Beethoven or this free unfolding of a word of ultimate sublimity and depth. We can only point to it fully conscious of the inadequacy of our words.

It is characteristic of this most conscious and objective of artists that he succeeded in encompassing everything in a work like the Ninth Symphony. The ninth is not exclusively a work of the late Beethoven, like the *Missa solemnis* or the late quartets; rather the entire Beethoven is embodied in it, all of the possibilities of the early, middle, and late Beethoven, though in a sublimation and intensification that was only possible for the later Beethoven. We do not hesitate to say: the Ninth Symphony of Beethoven is the work of art *par excellence*. Every note is a complete and brilliant inspiration, every detail as rich and meaningful in itself as it is perfect in its function within the whole. Form in the Ninth Symphony takes on such a unique inner significance that we can almost speak of an "ecstasy of form." An ultimate intensity and boundless fullness are regnant in the Ninth Symphony in every moment. And while everything is uttered in ultimate terms, said in a victoriously convincing way, leaving nothing behind, however small, that remains unrealized, nevertheless the dimension of infinity comes into view as otherwise never seen in art, and the radiance of eternity reveals itself like nowhere else in its portentous character of mystery.

The Beethovian art has the unique mission in humanity of serving as a wakeup call to recollection and going deeper, as an unrelenting condemnation of all philistine indolence, all mediocre half-heartedness as well as of all unseriousness and frivolity. It is a touchstone for everyone who perceives it with understanding, a touchstone for how awakened his spirit is for the world of values and for God, to what extent a value-responding posture asserts itself victoriously against habit, desensitization, and lazy self-indulgence. Beethoven's own development provides the model for resolving the special tasks of life's different phases. We do not find in him initially the dominance of the vital sphere, followed by the diminishing intensity in old age. No, with ever increasing intensity, the reverent purity, the tender trembling emotion and alertness of the young Beethoven is followed by a unique power and many-sidedness of the middle Beethoven, and finally by the mysterious serenity, ultimate spiritual depth, deepest recollection, the undivided turn to the Most High in the late Beethoven.

Beethoven's art represents a great examination of conscience for humanity. Woe to the time that seeks to flee from him and diminish him, the time that cannot bear his great and inexorable call to awake. Woe to the age that is ill at ease with his greatness and ultimate intensity and finds it tiresome. In so doing, it condemns itself. This is fundamentally true of any great and authentic art. A time that cannot bear or understand Beethoven understands Bach and Mozart just as little; for they do not stand antithetical to Beethoven but belong closely with him. Despite all their individual differences, the world of art is embodied in all three of them in such singular greatness and purity that it is impossible, even in the smallest point, to pit them against one another. Their differences are complementary in nature. Nevertheless it is not accidental that resistance to the "sursum corda" in true art of the highest kind is precisely directed above all against Beethoven. Bach and Mozart can be more easily mistaken in a purely technical and formalistic way. The "sursum corda" in them possesses a distance wherein the listener is not so relentlessly compelled to take a stance. But Beethoven is different! His call to awaken is of such extraordinary urgency that his meaning cannot be reinterpreted or fundamentally changed. From his art resounds the universal greeting: *tua res agitur* ("this concerns you"). And there is a deep reason for this, for the metaphysical situation of man is, as it were, embodied in Beethoven's art. His work is suffused with the one great yearning for God. His art speaks not of particular problems and difficulties; no, it speaks of the tragedy of mankind on earth as such and also of the indescribable joy of humanity in its ultimate destiny. Beethoven is truly a spokesman for humanity before God, and that which is uttered in his works is directed primarily to God and not to mankind. But this is precisely why his earnestness and ultimacy are an incomparable call for every person.

The person whose whole ethos is steeped in the desire for God, whose entire life is a great response to the radiant realm of values which proclaims God and draws us up to God, such a person's speech will be pervaded by the aura of God and he will speak to us of God. Thus Beethoven is not just a spokesman for humanity before God, but rather and above all a mouthpiece of God to humanity. In Beethoven's art, God speaks much more immediately to us than Beethoven's conscious intention encompassed. His art tells us much more about God than he himself perhaps knew of God. In this last point the consciousness of this most conscious of artists does not keep pace with his greatness. Hardly any other mass is as thoroughly Catholic as his *Missa solemnis*, even though many masses have been composed by other artists who personally lived much more deeply out of the supernatural. For no other artist has been so great and ultimate to be able to give such an adequate artistic expression of that which is greatest between heaven and earth, namely the Holy Mass, this event in which the ultimate fate of all humanity and of every individual person is at stake, no one so all-encompassing and in this sense "catholic" that he could function as spokesman for all of humanity. When at the beginning of the Benedictus the violin rings out, it is as if heaven bends down; when the Dona nobis pacem resounds, as if humanity from its true metaphysical position looks up beseechingly to God. Truly, if ever in the world of art the word applies, then here we must say: "It is the Passover of the Lord."

Franz Schubert

IN HIS MEMOIRS, SCHUBERT'S OLDEST FRIEND, the faithful Joseph von Spaun, describes the time during which they were both students at the Stadtkonvikt:

> One day Schubert sang for me a few little compositions based on poems by Klopstock. As I was very pleased with them, he looked trustingly into my eyes and asked, "Do you really think that something will become of me?" Assuring him that he had already accomplished a great deal, he replied, "I too think that something will come of me, but who is capable of accomplishing anything after Beethoven?"

Schubert's creative work flourished at an unusual moment—in the shadow of the towering figure of Beethoven. Although Schubert died a year after Beethoven, still he is Beethoven's first and truest heir. This does not mean that Schubert was not himself a genius with an entirely new artistic word to speak. On the contrary, an heir of Beethoven is one who, in an hour of unrepeatable fruitfulness—after the eruption of unheard-of new musical possibilities—could incarnate this unique musical situation in his own genius. This is why it seems so deeply and significantly symbolic that Schubert was one of the young men who had the honor, extraordinary and at once tragic, to accompany the king of music to the grave.

In my essay on Beethoven, I said that it was as if he created from the heart of all musical possibilities, uttering in every dimension the decisive and valid word.[1] We must recognize his unique place if we are to understand the incredibly stimulating, indeed exhilarating situation that arose through him in the realm of music. I said that Beethoven was in certain respects the greatest of all composers, and perhaps even the greatest of all artistic geniuses in every artistic domain. He was also the most influential of the great musical geniuses. (How slight is the influence of Bach and Mozart in comparison to him!) The great figures of the nineteenth century, whether Berlioz, Wagner, Brahms, or Bruckner, are all only possible as heirs of Beethoven.

Yet Schubert is the first and truest heir of Beethoven. Although musically he was part of a new generation, he dwelt in the same city alongside Beethoven; he listened, so to speak, to this pulse of music in itself; he received the spirit of Beethoven directly, even though he had little personal contact with him. It is against the colossal backdrop of Beethoven and the dramatic moment in music he embodied that we must see the wonder of this immensely gifted figure of Schubert—called to speak an entirely personal and thoroughly new word, a figure so uniquely loveable and filled with such extraordinary genius.

Schubert shares characteristics with Mozart: despite a short life, a fullness of compositions that can seem almost miraculous. Like Mozart, an extraordinary giftedness, an inexhaustible flow of ideas. Again like Mozart, an unfathomable, incomprehensible precociousness: Schubert composed *Gretchen am Spinnrad* when he was seventeen and *Erlkönig* when he was eighteen! And in Schubert and Mozart both, the genius of Austria dwells in a special way.

Then again, both in their lives and in their work, there are great contrasts. Mozart had a happy childhood. As a child prodigy, he was celebrated everywhere. At home, he lived in a milieu completely filled

---

1. See "Beethoven," 38, 38.

with music. His father encouraged his work and recognized his genius. Schubert, by contrast, found his father to be far less understanding. His father forbade the fifteen-year-old to compose and for a long time he was unable to forgive Schubert for having given up his position as a teacher. He did not have a piano in his parent's house and his father did not give him money to buy manuscript paper.

Later on, however, Mozart's life was especially difficult and lonely. Although his works were all performed, sometimes with success, no one besides Haydn grasped his unique and sublime greatness. Having no real friends, he died alone and no one accompanied his coffin. He was buried in a mass grave. And yet, his entire work is permeated by a unique joyfulness. His music always testifies to how splendid the world truly is; it is always filled with the spirit of *"pleni sunt coeli et terra gloria tua"*—"heaven and earth are full of your glory."

Schubert, on the other hand, had the rare good fortune of being surrounded by a circle of artistically stimulating friends, who fervently loved and revered him, who recognized his genius, and whom he in turn loved: Joseph von Spaun, Moritz von Schwind, Eduard von Bauernfeld, Anselm Hüttenbrenner, Franz von Schober—to mention only those with whom he was closest— as well as the great interpreter of Schubertian Lieder, Michael Vogl.[2] It is true that he did not have much luck with publishers, nor did his works always reach the general public, yet for all that he was surrounded by a group of friends, some of them people of stature, who loved and understood him, and his art was received with enthusiasm and understanding by a circle of cultured men and women. Through all the years of his short life, the "Schubertiaden," as they were called, took place—evenings which even Franz Grillparzer and Nikolaus von Lenau, Anastasius Grün and Ernst von Feuchtersleben often attended. And yet, Schubert's entire work is permeated by a deep melancholy—an understanding of the tragic dimension of human existence in this valley of tears—a presentiment of death.

2. [The German word "Lied" is often translated into English as "song." However, since the Lied in fact represents a particular genre within the more general category of the song, we have left Lied untranslated.—Trans.]

While both Mozart and Schubert died very young, Mozart's work is complete. One has the feeling that he gave his full measure. With Schubert, by contrast, the impression remains that he was taken away unfinished and that in the last years of his life he had attained a height that still contained a great future.

Yet despite the underlying tragic note, we find in Schubert a similar *coincidentia oppositorum* as in Beethoven and Mozart: Schubert too is capable of speaking in the most various voices and moods. On the one hand, there is the deeply tragic character as we find it in *Winterreise*, *Gretchen am Spinnrad*, *Der Wanderer*, and in the "Death and the Maiden" Quartet; on the other hand, the lovely cheerfulness and joy as we find in the Lieder *An Silvia* and *Alinde*, in the scherzo of the Octet, or in the "Trout" Quintet. It is interesting to compare Schubert's joyfulness with that of Mozart or Beethoven. It is neither the radiant, transfigured joy of Mozart, the "genius of light and love," nor is it the joy of Beethoven, which, as I said in my essay on Beethoven,[3] passes through the whole spectrum: from the high spirits of the closing movements of the Fifth and Sixth Quartets, opus 18, to the victoriously heroic joy of the Ninth Symphony. When Schubert is joyful, his joy is either of a fresh and natural character or it is lovely, sweet, and lyrical.

But the *coincidentia oppositorum* in Schubert reveals itself not only in the contrast of wistfulness and joyfulness. On the one hand, we find in many of his Lieder and sonatas, instead of the strict, taut form and conscious necessity of Beethoven, a musical "stroll," full of surprises; rather than the succinctness of Beethoven and Mozart, we find no hesitation about a certain lengthiness, about letting the music flow, like a poem by Eichendorff in comparison to a Shakespearean sonnet. On the other hand, we find in his chamber music, such as in the Octet or the C Major Quintet, a brilliant precision and masterful shaping to the very last detail. Another example: on the one hand, we find in the first theme of the C Major Quintet, in the scherzo of the Quartet opus 161, in the B-flat Major Trio, a sublime sweetness and humble loveliness—part joyful, part

---

3. See "Beethoven" 33–34.

wistful, but also permeated by a gentle humility, which must deeply move anyone with ears to hear. On the other hand, we find in the adagio from the C Major Quintet, the *Gruppe aus dem Tartarus*, the *Erlkönig*, the C Major Symphony and many others a grand power, an uncanny[4] (*dämonisch*) and mysterious character. Let us add that Schubert's sweetness and loveliness is not angelic, as in the case of Mozart, but specifically human, though this does not exclude it from being raised to the level of high sublimity. The power in the music of Schubert is totally different from that of Beethoven. There is a monumental power in Bach and especially in Beethoven. With Beethoven it is a power akin to Michelangelo, which is natural to him and grows organically out of the tremendous mountain of his personality. In Mozart, this aspect plays no role. In Schubert, however, we do find the specific element of power—but it is a "collected," an achieved power, to which he must rise through his artistic genius but which in no way flows naturally from his personality. It is the power of daemonic tension.

In Schubert we often find a folkish note [*Volkstümliche*], whether in Lieder such as *Heidenröslein, Der Lindenbaum, Das Echo*, or in many dances and marches. The fact that he always manages in such Lieder to avoid any kind of triviality, invariably a great danger in folk songs, is itself a special kind of genius. Yet the very same Schubert who can capture this folkish note, can also express one that is far removed from anything folklike, belonging to a solitary world of spirituality—such as the Lied *Suleika* or in his chamber music.

A prominent characteristic of Schubert's genius, alongside his gentle loveliness and grace, is the intimate. Neither Bach nor Beethoven are especially intimate, nor is this an aspect of either Mozart or Gluck's work. It is true that in Beethoven we find the characteristic of ultimate recollection and solitude. But the intimate in Schubert is not the result of the greatest recollection, nor does it appear only or even especially in the moments of greatest depth. One can also find it in works wherein a special loveliness and grace predominate. It is no accident that he be-

---

4. [When using the German word *dämonisch* in "Schubert," Hildebrand does not mean demonic or diabolical but rather a sense of the uncanny and darkly mysterious.—Trans.]

came the creator and master of the Lied, which, like the poem, is by its very nature an especially intimate artistic form. Yet in contrast to other composers of Lieder who came after him, the intimate in Schubert is marked by a specific chasteness and humility.

The *coincidentia oppositorum* in Schubert shows itself in yet another way: that sometimes he is Romantic, sometimes Classical; in one moment Romantic, in the next quite un-Romantic.

In my essay on Beethoven, I distinguished three senses of the word "Romantic." The first has a purely historical sense and the second refers to particular characteristic features, which imply neither a value nor a disvalue. By contrast, the third sense refers to the phenomenon of a certain artistic decomposition, which is to say that it has the taint of disvalue.[5] Schubert is never Romantic in the third and negative sense; but, in contrast to Beethoven, he is undoubtedly Romantic in the second sense of the word. The characteristics of Romantic in this sense—the picturesque charm rather than monumental construction, the looser form, the new relationship to nature, and many others—find a wonderful and genuinely artistic expression in Schubert. They all belong to the special "word" entrusted to him by God. Far from being at odds with the purity and height of his art, these elements constitute a fully legitimate aspect in the world of art. To set this sense of the Romantic negatively against the Classical is just as absurd as considering Baroque architecture an artistic degeneration to be set at odds with Renaissance or Gothic architecture.

We have still said little about Schubert if we characterize his art as Romantic, even in this positive sense. We have only to think of Schubert's contemporary, Carl Maria von Weber, who is also a Romantic in the positive sense of the term, to see how Schubert is definitely not always and exclusively a Romantic. Weber is only a Romantic. His masterpiece, *Der Freischütz*, is completely filled with Romanticism—in its fragrance, its purity and morning freshness. All of Weber's other works are also Romantic, including *Euryanthe* and *Oberon*. If Schubert in many of his Lieder speaks as a Romantic, then there are also Lieder, such as *An*

---

5. See "Beethoven," p. 25.

Silvia, Im Grünen, An die Nachtigall, Ganymed, Der Hirt auf dem Felsen, Sehnsucht, Gruppe aus dem Tartarus, and above all *Suleika*, which are completely un-Romantic.

Through all the layers of Schubert's art, from the peripheral and lighter to those of mysterious greatness, runs the trait of an indescribable loveliness [*Anmut*]. We find it in the marches and dances, in *Die schöne Müllerin*, and in *Rosamunde*. It appears in the piano sonatas, in the "Trout" Quintet, in the Octet, in the B-flat Major Trio and the C Major Quintet: always a gentle loveliness, permeated by the incomparable beauty of humility and tenderness. The connection of this loveliness with the mysterious power and uncanny depth [*dämonischen Tiefe*] in his greatest works is perhaps the very heart of the Schubertian genius.

We mentioned above the specifically Austrian note in Schubert. He is not just a special incarnation of the Austrian essence, in its grace, humility, wistfulness, and loveliness; he is also in a very special way bound up with Vienna, the city which he so deeply loved. Robert Schumann wrote in his essay on Schubert's C Major Symphony:

> "It is true, that this Vienna—with its St. Stephen's Cathedral, its beautiful women, its splendid public spaces, and the way in which it stretches into the flowering landscape, surrounded by the Danube as if by countless ribbons, and rising gradually into the increasingly higher mountains—this Vienna with all of its reminders of the greatest German masters must be a fruitful soil for the imagination of the musician. In Schubert's symphony, with its bright and burgeoning life, the city stands before my mind's eye today more clearly than ever before and it again becomes quite clear to me how such works could be born in just this kind of environment."

And the twenty-one year old Schubert wrote from Zseliz, in Hungary, to his brother Ferdinand: "Yes, beloved Vienna, within your narrow confines you hold what is dearest and loveliest." Schubert was in many respects a son of Vienna. He possessed the Viennese *joie de vivre*, a certain lightheartedness, grace in enjoyment, amiability, and gaiety. This comes to expression in his dances, marches, and in certain Lieder.

In this connection we must be clear about the double-aspect of the Vienna in which Schubert lived. On the one hand, there is the Vienna of the Biedermeier period, the Vienna of Romanticism, full of the charm of life, of gaiety, of cultural ferment, the Vienna of Ferdinand Raymund and Johann Nestroy, the Vienna of Joseph Lanner and the father of Johann Strauss, Jr., the Vienna of Franz Grillparzer and Nikolaus Lenau, the Vienna in which Adalbert Stifter studied, the Vienna in which in 1823 Weber's *Euryanthe* was performed. On the other hand, there is also the Vienna in which Beethoven lived, in which in 1814 *Fidelio* was performed in its present-day version, in which in 1824 the Ninth Symphony rang out for the first time—the Vienna in which Beethoven's tremendous call to awaken rang out with its ultimate seriousness.

Schubert was deeply bound up with both of these worlds. On the one hand, he stands at the center of the Vienna of the Romantic period. When one of Schubert's quartets for male voices was performed, Nestroy sang the bass part and Carl Maria von Weber was present at the concert. As already mentioned, Grillparzer and Lenau belonged to Schubert's circle—as did Anastasius Grün, Ernst von Feuchtersleben, the painters Josef Danhauser and Leopold Kupelwieser. This circle of friends really shared a common life. They met at the Schubertiaden, where the newly composed works of Schubert were awaited with the greatest excitement and received with enthusiasm. They gathered at Schober's, where they read Kleist's dramas and Heine's poetry. They made excursions in horse-drawn carriages into the uniquely beautiful environs of Vienna, and they were hospitably received in the villas of the Bruchmann family in Hütteldorf and in the beautiful little Atzenbrugg castle. Delicious meals were served. They danced. (Schubert himself did not dance, but he played for the dance!) And regularly, the friends gathered with Schubert in the Gasthaus zum grünen Anker in Grünangergasse, and in the Gasthaus zum Stern, in Brandstett, in Grinzing just outside of Vienna.

How many Lieder Schubert composed with friends or by himself in inns! "One evening," Anselm Hüttenbrenner recounts:

I invited Schubert since I had received several bottles of red wine from a respected house as a gift for having served as accompanist on several occasions. After we had drunk the noble Sexarder to the last drop, Schubert sat down at my desk and composed the wonderfully lovely Lied, *Die Forelle*, which I still possess in the original. When he was almost finished and already tired, he accidentally poured ink instead of the blotting sand so that several measures became almost illegible.

On another occasion, Schubert came to pick up Schwind for a walk. The latter, however, could not part from the drawing on which he was working and, to keep his songful friend from leaving, urged him to compose. Though having to draw his own lines and lacking a text, which he then found in Shakespeare's *Cymbeline*, he composed *Horch, horch die Lerch' im Ätherblau*.

In order to understand the height and depth of Schubert's genius, we cannot see him only in the light of his stimulating and lively circle of friends, which surrounded him and organized the Schubertiaden—not just in the light of the Vienna of Romanticism. This is just one side of Schubert's spirit, reflected in some of his Lieder and other works. In his most authentic works—in Lieder such as *Suleika* and *Gruppe aus dem Tartarus*, in the B Minor Symphony, the C Major Symphony, and above all in his incomparable chamber music—we encounter a Schubert who far surpasses this circle, who leads us into a solitary, sublime world wherein he stands as Beethoven's first great heir. It is the Schubert who said of himself: "At times it seems to me that I do not even belong in this world"; it is the Schubert who breathes the air of the Vienna that is filled with Beethoven's work.

Beethoven was for Schubert the musical ideal. Admittedly, he also had a great love for Handel, and Gluck's *Iphigenie en Tauride* impressed him deeply. Schubert, who was otherwise so gentle, once almost came to blows in a tavern with a university professor who made fun of a performance of *Iphigenie*. And what Mozart meant to Schubert is expressed in the words I quoted in my essay on Mozart: "Oh Mozart, immortal

Mozart, how many, how infinitely many such consoling imprints of a luminous, better life have you impressed upon our souls!"

But his relationship to Beethoven, in whose shadow he lived, was still on a completely different plane. We already mentioned Schubert's remark, "but who can really do anything after Beethoven?" One day when he was hastily departing from school, he read at the Kärntnertor the announcement for the performance of *Fidelio* and sold his books to get a ticket for the performance. The twenty-year old Schubert noted on the copy he had purchased of *Ich liebe Dich so wie Du mich*, written in Beethoven's own hand: "In the handwriting of the immortal Beethoven, obtained August 14, 1817." And on an empty page of the manuscript, he immediately wrote a composition inspired by the thought of Beethoven.

To the writer, Braun von Braunthal, however, Schubert said of Beethoven:

> He can do everything; we, however, cannot yet grasp everything, and much water will flow through the Danube before what this man has created will become widely understood. He is the most sublime and most fertile of all musical poets.

How Schubert, despite the limited personal contact with Beethoven, lived continually in a milieu filled with the presence of the master whom he loved and revered above all else, is illustrated in the following episode recounted by Anselm Hüttenbrenner:

> A few times a week, between eleven and twelve o'clock, Beethoven would come into the bookshop of the publisher Steiner & Co. Almost every time, there was a gathering of composers and an exchange of musical opinions. Schubert frequently accompanied me. We delighted in Beethoven's earthy and sometimes sarcastic remarks.

There is a musical genre of which Schubert is the real creator, namely the Lied. In his Lieder, Schubert created an entirely new type of relationship between the spoken word and music, thereby establishing for the Lied an analogous place in the realm of music as the poem possesses in the realm of literature. One can hardly speak of the Lied with Bach,

Gluck, or Handel, and in the case of Haydn and Mozart it represents a minor artistic genre, incomparable in importance with their other compositions. One has only to compare Mozart's arias with his Lieder, which are more like occasional poems than fully realized works of lyrical poetry, to ascertain the relative modesty of his Lieder writing. Certainly, the Lieder of Beethoven took on an entirely new and significant form of their own; think of *Kennst du das Land*, *Herz mein Herz*, *Adelaide*, and, above all, *An die ferne Geliebte*, which in certain respects is the most beautiful Lied ever written. But even with Beethoven, the Lied as a whole remains secondary as an art form, incomparable in significance with his symphonies and sonatas, with his chamber music, and his sacred music. With Schubert, by contrast, the Lied becomes a fully artistic genre. The way in which music and poetry are united, the way in which sound and word interpenetrate into a perfect unity, is something completely new. His Lieder are musical poems. They unfold a kind of poetic charm in music that can only be found in this artistic form.

Furtwängler rightly stresses that the ideal basis for a Lied is not the poem that is already perfect in itself. In the most beautiful Goethe poems, he says, the best musical composition is often not an intensification of the final impression. The music certainly adds something new—but the whole in its final effect is not necessarily more beautiful or more significant than the poem on its own.

Consequently, even among the Schubert Lieder based on Goethe poems we must distinguish between two types. Of the most perfect poems, such as *Gretchen am Spinnrad* or *Ganymed*, one cannot say that the Lied is greater than the poems on their own. Yet it is something new and wonderful that comes about when the music allows itself to be lifted up by the poem and when, through its very own powers, the music adequately expresses the world of the poem and the original experience at the root of the poem. The musical work as such is therefore a great artistic enrichment for art, even if it is not an enhancement of the poem. Something analogous occurs in the case of Verdi's masterpiece, *Otello*; in the final impression, the opera is not richer, greater or more beautiful that the spoken *Othello* of Shakespeare, but we must thank God that we possess this wonderful and tremendous music drama of Verdi, which in a remarkable way is filled with Shakespeare's spirit. In Lieder such as *Gretchen am Spinnrad* and *Ganymed*, the extraordinary genius of Schubert shows itself precisely in the fact that he can be so great and original even while standing in a supporting relation to the poem.

The case is different with the *Erlkönig* or with Marianne von Willemer's poem *Suleika*, which is completely inspired by the spirit of Goethe. Here the Lied towers above the poem in the final impression. The poem is admittedly of great beauty, but not of the sort of perfection that excludes a musical enhancement of the final effect. The Schubertian Lied *Suleika* is therefore incomparably greater than the poem, even if it is one in spirit with the poem.

Apart from the question whether the Lied is greater and more powerful than poetry as such, we must distinguish among different basic types in Schubert's Lieder with regard to the role of music and the spoken word. When the poems possess a strong, potent inner world of their own, Schubert in his music enters into this special world in such a way that the Lied becomes, as it were, one with the spirit of the poet. This is just as true for a Lied like *An Silvia*, which in its overall effect transcends the poem, as it is for *Ganymed*, which remains still greater as a poem. *An Silvia* breathes a distinctively Shakespearean world—the universality of Shakespeare—the unique, graceful poetry of *The Two Gentlemen of Verona*. Similarly, *Ganymed* is completely suffused by the spirit of Goethe. *Suleikas Erster Gesang*, perhaps the most perfect of all Schubert's Lieder, not only fully expresses the spirit of Goethe but also in a special manner the world of the *Westöstlicher Divans*.[6] In these Lieder one is primarily transported into the world of the poet, even if entirely by musical means. This capacity to incarnate musically the spirit of the poet in a fully original way is the sign of a unique genius.

In a second type of Schubert-Lied, the music actualizes much that only potentially exists in the poem. The world of the poet recedes here

---

6. [*West-Eastern Divan*, a collection of poems by Goethe, from which Schubert set the poem "Suleika."—Trans.]

as that of Schubert emerges more prominently. Yet the atmosphere of the poem still has a strong influence on the whole, even if more that of a stimulus for Schubert's genius. Furtwängler's statement is especially applicable here: "With Schubert the music absorbs the words into its flow." This second type includes Lieder such as *Du bist die Ruh*, with the text of Friedrich Rückert, the lovely Lied *Die linden Lüfte sind erwacht*, with Ludwig Uhland's text, and above all, the two wonderful Lieder based on poems by Schiller, the unique *Sehnsucht* and the magnificent *Gruppe aus dem Tartarus*. Also belonging to this type are the Lieder based on poetry by Matthias Claudius: the wonderful *Der Tod und das Mädchen* and *Am Grabe Anselmos*.

In a third type of Lied, Schubert elevates a poem that is in itself insignificant into a completely new world formed by him alone. The new unity of the music and the spoken word can also be found here. Indeed, the words become beautiful and poetic through the music.

The abundance of different voices, moods, and sensibilities in which Schubert speaks in his Lieder is inexhaustible—whether a folklike simplicity, as in *Der Lindenbaum* or *Heidenröslein*, full of innocent charm and a natural poetry; the note of a fresh morning-like mood of life, as in several of the Lieder on poems by Wilhelm Müller; the character of the Romantic spiritualization of nature, as in the *Erlkönig*; or a deep melancholy and presentiment of death, as in *Der Wegweiser* and *Die Krähe*; the element of the uncanny, as in the *Der Doppelgänger*; the mature, spiritual, and sublime lyricism, as in *Suleika*; the highest Goethean poetry of nature, as in *Ganymed*—particularly in the words "Lieblicher Morgenwind!/Ruft drein die Nachtigall" ("Lovely morning breeze! The nightingale calls"); the passionate ardor, the supreme tragedy of the figure of Gretchen in *Faust* in the Lied *Gretchen am Spinnrad*; the barren tragic irony, as in *Der Leiermann*; the contemplative poetry of nature, as in Schiller's *Sehnsucht*. What a tremendous range between *An Silvia* and *Du bist die Ruh*, between *Die Forelle* and *Der Wegweiser*, or between *An die Musik* and *Die Krähe*—each one so beautiful and deeply poetic. Or what difference between the magnificent world of the *Gruppe aus dem*

Tartarus and the sweet gentleness of *Die Nachtigall* or *Alinde*. In all of this we see how universal Schubert is.

Schubert had a very special relationship to nature. The beauty of nature, particularly the region surrounding Vienna, was one of his primary sources of joy. In his Lieder we find a completely new relationship of music to nature. The magic of a brook is rendered in an incomparable manner in the Lied *Ich hört' ein Bächlein rauschen*, the blowing of the wind in the *Erlkönig*, the world of snow and ice in *Der Leiermann*. We are not thinking of an imitative rendition of nature and certain sounds heard in nature, which we already find early in the history of music, also often in Haydn; rather we are thinking of the atmosphere of the elements of nature and their specifically poetic content, which Schubert places before our imagination. This is a new role of the elements of nature in music, which is also to be found in Wagner in a unique manner.

It has often been pointed out that the accompaniment in Schubert's Lieder acquires an entirely different significance than it previously possessed in the Lied. Indeed, this belongs essentially to his re-invention of the Lied. The accompaniment is not just an innocuous supplement to the sung melody, but possesses a relationship to the poem in its own right. It builds up the world and the specific poetry of the words out of its own resources. In so doing, it acquires a significance analogous to the orchestra in Wagner's music dramas.

The function of the accompaniment is not just one of pure imitation of natural sounds. Certainly, we also find in it an imitative rendering of the brook, the wind, and so forth. But it would be completely wrong to think that the relationship of the accompaniment to the content of the poem was exhausted in this. It is not this merely imitative reproduction of an object of which the poem speaks. The mere fact that we are reminded of a brook, of the wind, of the rustling of leaves would neither suffice to establish a poetic world, nor would it come about by musical means, but would amount to little more than the stimulation of the listener's imagination. The greatness and uniqueness of Schubert's Lieder accompaniment lies rather in the fact that with purely musical means and beyond all musical imitation he is able to present directly the true poetry and beauty of nature—and often far beyond what the poet was able achieve, as for example in *Die schöne Müllerin* and in *Die Winterreise*. The music in fact opens new dimensions of beauty and poetry in the elements of nature; analogous to the true lyric poem, the music reveals deeper layers of the poetry of nature. That the accompaniment is not merely an imitation of natural sounds can be seen in a Lied such as *Gretchen am Spinnrad*. The exceptional element of Schubert's creation is not that the Lied reminds us of a spinning wheel; rather it is the contrast between the relentless advance in the accompaniment to the drama of the voice, the special poetry of the accompaniment, its interruption, its hesitant resumption.

The river of Schubertian Lieder (which fills six volumes), flows inexhaustibly, continually offers new surprises, even though, of course, there are great differences in beauty and significance within this river. Just as wonderful as the inexhaustibility of this river, as the richness of Schubert's many voices and moods, and as the wide range between the various worlds embodied by the Lieder, is the genius with which the poems are penetrated in certain Lieder, especially when the poem is of unusual grandeur.

One must grasp the utter moving greatness of the poetry in *Gretchen am Spinnrad* to appreciate the unique achievement of Schubert's Lied based on that poem. What resounds in "Meine Ruh ist hin" ("My peace is lost") are primordial human words, expressing in overwhelming simplicity and intensity the ancient tragedy of human destiny. No one receptive to truly great poetry can read this poem with dry eyes. And how uniquely did Schubert, at the age of only seventeen, compose this Lied! What inspiration in the accompaniment which reproduces the spinning wheel, what a dramatic ascent to the words "Und ach, sein Kuss!" ("And Oh, his kiss!"). And then the halting resumption of the accompaniment.

In the two Lieder-cycles, *Die schöne Müllerin* and *Winterreise*, Schubert created a completely new artistic genre: a musical epic, a series of Lieder capable of standing on their own, yet successively telling a story, which as a whole form a unity. This artistic genre offers entirely new possibilities of an artistic kind, which Schubert developed and realized in a unique way. It is a loosely joined whole, leaving the individual Lieder their full freedom, and yet a unified, continuous stream which spreads before our minds a particular overall atmosphere.

The text of *Die schöne Müllerin* is modest; but in Schubert's Lieder cycle, an incomparable world of poetic charm arises, which makes also the poetry precious and loveable. What inexhaustible invention, what overflowing inspiration, filled with the charm of the Schubertian spirit. All the "ups" and "downs" in the anticipation of happiness, hope, love, pain, and wistfulness unfolds before us. What a stirring cry in "Der Mai is kommen, der Winter is aus" ("May has come and winter is over"). What a lovely, moving murmur in the lullaby of the brook.

If Schubert's wonderful, lyrical grace unfolds in *Die schöne Müllerin*, then in *Winterreise* we encounter the other side of Schubert: the daemonic and uncanny. This second Lieder-cycle is incomparably more significant than *Die schöne Müllerin*. Lieder such as *Im Dorfe* and *Der Wegweiser* not only rise to a greater musical beauty and depth, but the entire work possesses a much more intense and concentrated character. Certainly, even here we find folklike Lieder, like *Der Lindenbaum*. Yet the majority of the Lieder have a taut structure and a compact power, especially the last Lied, *Der Leiermann*. Spaun reports how Schubert said one day:

> "Come today to Schober's, and I will sing for you a cycle of Lieder that will make you shudder. I am eager to hear what you all will say. They have affected me more than was ever the case with any other Lieder." He then sang for us, in a voice filled with emotion, the entire *Winterreise*. We were completely taken aback by the somber mood of the Lieder, and Schober said that he only liked one Lied, *Der Lindenbaum*. Schubert said only: "I like these Lieder more than any others, and you will still come to like them." And he was right. The impression of these wistful Lieder, masterfully performed by Vogl, soon made us enthusiastic. They were his true swansong.

Despite the overall atmosphere of these Lieder-cycles, within them are great differences in the beauty, power, and depth of the individual Lieder.

The relationship between music and the spoken word in the Lied is completely different from that in opera—as different as plays are from poems. Just as the talent that makes someone a great playwright does not necessarily guarantee that he will create great poems, and vice versa, the same is also true with respect to the Lied and opera. Hölderlin, Germany's greatest lyric poet after Goethe, was not a playwright, any more than Kleist was a lyricist. In opera—whether in *Fidelio, Figaro, Don Giovanni*, or in Wagner's *Tristan und Isolde* or *Die Meistersinger*—the music fashions the characters. The people who move about and act on the stage are themselves singing and the music becomes an expression of their being. The music moreover forms the entire dramatic situation that we see and experience on the stage. All of this is entirely absent in the case of the Lied. Here the music unites itself with the completely self-enclosed poetic world of the poem, which does not present itself as reality, as is the case with drama, and does not unfold before us but rather allows us to peer into a world of its own as if through a window. While in one respect the interpenetration of word and music in opera is more radical, in another it is more intimate and detailed in the Lied.

Unfortunately, we cannot go into all the kinds of "absolute music" in Schubert's work, but can only briefly point out various things. Schubert's piano music occupies a very special place within his work. It is a further sign of his power and profoundly original spirit that he, Beethoven's heir, was able to develop a completely different aspect of the piano from Beethoven's. Of course, his sonatas cannot be compared with those of Beethoven with respect to beauty, power, and depth. But then he never aspired to anything analogous. From Schubert the piano received an entirely different and thoroughly new function, and within this framework he created works of great beauty and special charm. His style of piano music also had an extraordinary influence on the piano literature of the nineteenth century. In his music for four hands, he created a virtually new genre of piano music. From among these many works I mention only the wonderful, mysterious fantasy in G Major, which represents something unique in the piano literature.

It should therefore not surprise us that the king of the Lied, despite many efforts, did not create any operas or singspiels that were able to establish themselves. In all, he composed eighteen works for the stage. Even on his deathbed, he was still occupied with the idea of his opera, *Graf von Gleichen*, for which his friend Bauernfeld had written the text. Yet not only did his stage works fail to succeed, they are also incomparable in significance with his other works. This is why the most beautiful elements of his operas are usually the overtures or the incidental music—as with *Rosamunde*—which is to say, the portions that are "absolute music."

Schubert began composing symphonies already at the age of sixteen. While the first three are still relatively minor, he had already composed the so-called "Tragic" Symphony and the Fifth Symphony at the age of nineteen. They are wonderful works, full of beautiful ideas and with a noble poetic world. Yet they do not yet carry the full stamp of Schubert's character, and consequently they have been jokingly dubbed the "Haydn-Mozart" symphonies. His full individuality already expresses itself much more strongly in *Gretchen am Spinnrad* and the *Erlkönig*, Lieder he composed two years earlier. Yet even here we find the unfathomable precociousness and giftedness of Schubert, who was so young when he wrote these two early symphonies, which in no way exhibit the character of imitation or derivation but are full of genuine inspiration—works which fully established themselves.

Surprisingly, his Sixth Symphony, written at age twenty-one, is not as significant as these. But in the year 1822, when he was twenty-five, that mature and wonderful work of genius, the Symphony in B Minor, dubbed the "Unfinished," came into being. Schubert stands before us here in his full power, for this work is filled through and through with his unique genius. What restrained power in the opening theme, which then progresses with such insistent murmuring. What grace in the second theme, which, especially in the recapitulation, expands victoriously, like a view into a luminous world. And how rich and inspired the mysterious second movement is!

What Schubert was and could have become as a symphonist had he been granted a longer life is made clear by the C Major Symphony, which he composed in the last year of his life when he was thirty-one.

This masterpiece, which reveals Schubert in his nobility, in all his power and greatness, was, as is well known, only found by Schumann among his belongings ten years after his death and was subsequently performed for the first time in Leipzig.

Sacred music also occupies a substantial place in Schubert's work. All told, he wrote seven masses, though only the last one in E-flat Major, written in his final year, reaches the height of his very great and most characteristic works. I would like to draw particular attention to the Incarnatus which, in its gentle, serenely advancing rhythm represents something entirely new compared with the mystical, mysterious Incarnatus of the *Missa Solemnis* of Beethoven and the contemplative, angelic Incarnatus of Mozart's C Minor Mass. If we prescind from the two greatest ones—that of Beethoven and Mozart—this is the most beautiful Incarnatus in the entire musical literature.

Also unique in the whole of sacred music is the interweaving of the Incarnatus and the Crucifixus. First three voices, two tenors and a soprano, alternatingly sing the incomparable Incarnatus, followed by the magnificent Crucifixus with the ominous trumpet. Then, the Incarnatus resounds again, sung this time by the soprano, followed again by the Crucifixus. This is an entirely unique conception, which, as it were, allows us to see the mystery of the incarnation in light of the crucifixion. Another highpoint in this mass is the Dona nobis pacem, again with a wonderful theme, sacred, moving, urgent. Here the deeply Catholic element in Schubert reveals itself.

But the pinnacle of his work is undoubtedly to be found in his chamber music. Already the "Trout" Quintet, composed when he was twenty-two, is filled with irresistible charm. Here the daemonic mysteriousness, the power of the later chamber music, does not yet emerge. Rather it is the element of an indescribable gracefulness and lovely poetry that bears witness to the fact that Schubert's genius manifests itself with supreme power and intensity in the sphere of chamber music. The same is true to an even greater extent of the Quartettsatz, which he composed when he was twenty-three years old. What an extraordinary work! And what musical gems the two wonderful quartets are, the one in A Minor the other in D Minor with its variations on the Lied, *Der Tod und das Mädchen*. Yet what we encounter in the Octet, the B-flat Major Trio, the Quartet opus 161, and the Quintet in C Major is still incomparably greater.

Some mistakenly believe that the apex of Schubert's work lies in his Lieder. But as incomparable and as original as he is as a Lieder composer—as much as he is the actual creator of this genre—it would be wrong to glimpse in them the peak of Schubertian music. Inexhaustible as the world of poetic magic is that emerges in his Lieder, in these chamber music works Schubert reaches a mysterious depth and intensity that show him as far greater and more sublime. It is a special mark of his genius that he, who was inspired in a special way by the spoken word, who in his Lieder entered into the spirit of the poems like no other—that he, the master of the Lied, nevertheless rises to unimagined heights when he can follow his musical inspiration alone, like in these chamber works.

What a world of rich, moving, profound genius and extraordinary poetry stands before us in the Octet. A masterpiece of breathtaking genius, a world of its own, in which the various aspects of Schubert's genius fully unfold themselves. The originality of the ideas, the richness in harmonic changes, the Schubertian transitions between major and minor, a pastoral poetry, like Giorgione's painting, *Concert Champêtre*, the lovely humility and the foreboding mystery—all of this comes to expression here. The splendid theme at the beginning of the first movement breathes an air of momentous mysteriousness. In the subsequent themes in the course of this movement, an epic depth and a stimulating genius unfold before us; a poetry that surpasses even that of all the Lieder and which is not Romantic but truly Classical. What a great contemplative musical line in the second movement, in which resounds one of the noblest and most beautiful melodies ever written. What soulful music, at the same time so filled with the moods of nature, so chaste, so intense! And in the middle of the movement, what intensification and expressivity in the second theme. What enchanting pastoral poetry in the third movement, what delightful high spirits; and in the fifth, what moving loveliness, what supremely poetic liveliness, full of love, purity, and humility; and in the final movement again the mysteriously tragic and uncanny. In the Octet, we find a world full of exalted beauty and inner necessity, of brilliant precision and inexhaustible abundance. Truly, if Schubert had written nothing other than the Octet, he would have been one of the greatest musicians!

Alongside the Octet, the Quartet opus 161, composed in 1826, represents the pinnacle of the quartets. The first movement with its extraordinary intensity and genius is also filled with Schubert's mysterious and daemonic character. The andante is perhaps the most beautiful movement. It opens with one of those Schubertian themes in which is held both a sublime loveliness and moving humility. The way this theme unfolds in ever new harmonic transformations, sounding at one moment high in the violin, and especially at the end when it is continually being developed and transformed anew, sometimes in major, sometimes in minor, is of incomparable beauty. The trio in the scherzo is also full of sublimity. Its gently ambling movement belongs to a type of themes which we also encounter now and then in the symphonies of Bruckner. Sometimes these themes are considered to be dance-like in a "Viennese" sort of way. Yet this seems to me to be a great mistake. These themes, rather, have a hovering sublime character, and the theme of this scherzo represents a highpoint of the special grace, moving loveliness, and sweetness of Schubert.

And what can I say of the B-flat Major Trio, with its wonderful first movement, beginning full of brio and then leading into one of those special Schubertian themes of mysterious wistfulness. The climax is the adagio, in which a word of stirring beauty is spoken, a world of noble, pure urgency, as simple as it is deep, as pure as it is filled with a contemplative recollection. What a gentle, sweet farewell at the end of the movement. Yet in the last movement as well, after the fresh, graceful introduction, an extraordinary passage of sudden recollectedness, a lingering in the depths with a tragic undertone.

Perhaps the peak of his entire work is the Quintet in C Major, which he wrote immediately before his death. Here, as it were, all Schubert's various traits come to expression in highest perfection. In the first movement, a recollected power, and then in the main theme, a gracefulness and beautiful humility. The adagio is perhaps the most mysterious thing Schubert wrote: in the first part, a sublime weaving and a hovering full of anticipation, and then the daemonically dark part full of compressed power. What a display of genius in the scherzo. The last movement offers a great surprise: a blossoming theme overflowing with *joie de vivre*, perhaps the most joyous of Schubertian themes, and then again a magnificent theme with that same contemplative lingering and tragic undertone.

Schubert is a particularly moving figure, with his God-given talent, on the one hand, his unique modesty, on the other. At the Schubertiaden he often declined to accompany his own Lieder and only turned the pages or sat far off in the background. When his *Tod und das Mädchen* Quartet was performed for the first time at one of these Schubertiaden, the first violinist said, "Little brother, better stick to your Lieder. This is nothing." Without a word, Schubert packed up the music and left this unique work lying in a drawer. Shortly before his death, after he had written the C Major Symphony, the E-flat Major Mass, and the sublime Quintet in C Major, he enrolled at the conservatory to study counterpoint and music theory with Simon Sechter.

Often we even encounter a great timidity in Schubert. At the performance of his opera *Die Zwillingsbrüder* he sat with a friend in the background. The opera—actually more of an operetta—was a great success and the audience enthusiastically called for Schubert to come out. He would not budge from the box where he was seated, because he was wearing his old jacket and did not wish to be seen in it. When a friend offered to exchange the old coat for his own dress coat, Schubert found other excuses. He did not appear for the first performance of *Erlkönig*, and often he had to be pulled out of a restaurant or a coffee shop to attend a Schubertiade.

This shyness also showed itself in his first meeting with Beethoven. In 1822, when he was twenty-five, Schubert brought Beethoven his variations for four hands, which he had also dedicated to him. When Beethoven expressed the wish that Schubert write down the answers to Schubert's own questions, his hand became as if handcuffed. Beethoven looked through the composition and came across a harmonic mistake, which he gently pointed out to Schubert, adding that it was not a fatal error. Schubert, however, completely lost his composure and only after he had left the house was he able to pull himself together. He never again had the courage to present himself to the master—not until the year 1827, when Beethoven was already very sick.[7] Here we see alongside his shyness his deep reverence for Beethoven.

Schubert's great modesty and bashfulness is also evident in the way he would raise his hands dismissively when his music was being praised. At a gathering where many of his Lieder were sung, he said: "Now enough of this, I'm getting bored." On the other hand, when on one occasion he heard something he had written a long time ago, he was amazed that it was by him, and with genuine objectivity exclaimed that he had not thought he had composed something so beautiful. Anselm Hüttenbrenner recounts: "If I praised a Lied especially, he would reply, 'Yes, it's just a good poem, so something good immediately comes to mind—the melodies come pouring in, making it a real joy.'"

Kathi Fröhlich, a friend of Grillparzer, said of Schubert: "He was never envious and ill-tempered. On the contrary, what joy he had when some beautiful piece of music was performed. He would put his hands together and to his mouth and sit there completely enraptured." And Spaun said of him: "His character was incredibly trusting and open, friendly and grateful—open in his joys, reserved in his sorrows." How beautiful are the words Schubert himself wrote in his diary: "High spirits, heavy heart. Excessive high spirits usually hide a very heavy heart."

Also typical of Schubert was the scant attentiveness he showed toward his own works. When good friends came to him, they would often carry off notebooks, promising to return them, which they seldom did. Often Schubert did not know who had carried off this or that Lied. His friend Josef Hüttenbrenner attempted laboriously to collect everything—a hundred Lieder in all. Just as he was lavishly gifted by God, just as the river of his ideas lavishly overflowed, so also was his attitude toward others with respect to his own works.

7. [This passage is virtually a quotation from *Beethoven as I Knew Him* by Beethoven's first biographer, Anton Schindler. Hildebrand seems to have been attempting to paraphrase.—Trans]

And yet for all of his modesty, a deep awareness of his artistic mission dwelt in him—of the word God had entrusted him to speak. Thus he once said to a group of orchestra musicians, who declared that they were artists like himself: "I am Schubert. I have done great things and will do even greater things, for I am not merely a composer of *Ländler*,[8] as it is written in the silly newspapers and as silly people repeat."

The refined Anton Ottenwalt had this to say about Schubert's noble mind:

> We sat up until shortly before midnight and never have I seen him like this ... How seriously, profoundly, how enthusiastically he spoke about art, poetry, his youth and his friends, about other significant people, and the relationship of the ideal to life. I had to marvel more and more at this spirit.

But it is not only Schubert the human being who is a moving and loveable figure. His art, too, has an especially moving and deeply loveable note. Liszt has captured this in these wonderful words:

> O restlessly welling, lovable genius—harmony, freshness, power, loveliness, fervor, succor, tears and flames stream from the height and depth of your heart; you almost allow the greatness of your mastery to be forgotten because of the magical charm of your spirit.

The inexpressible, lovely gracefulness, the poetry of nature, the sublime beauty of humility that lives in his melodies, the deep tragedy that permeates his art, the mysterious, daemonic power: against the background of his gentle and modest personality, all this is extraordinarily moving and loveable.

We stand deeply moved and full of loving reverence in the presence of such God-given talent, which seems to us miraculous. How we can understand Moritz von Schwind, who at the end of his life said that of all things his hand had ever drawn, the most valuable were a few empty music lines that he once drew for Schubert in the absence of music paper

---

8. [An Austrian folk dance.—Trans.]

and which, barely dry, were permitted to capture Schubertian melodies. Beethoven's biographer, Anton Schindler, recounts:

> Since the sickness, to which Beethoven finally succumbed after four months of suffering, made his customary intellectual activity impossible from the onset of his illness, one had to think of a distraction for him in accord with his mind and inclination. So it happened that I presented him with a compilation of Lieder and other vocal music by Schubert, about sixty in all, many still in manuscript form. The great master, who previously had known not five of Schubert's Lieder, was amazed at their number and could not believe that Schubert had already written more than five hundred by that time (February 1827). Yet if he marveled over their number, he was utterly astonished when he discovered their content. For several days he could not part with them at all, and for hours on end he lingered daily over Iphigenia's Monologue, the *Grenzen der Menschheit*, *Die Allmacht*, the *Die junge Nonne*, *Viola*, *Die schöne Müllerin*, and others. With joyful enthusiasm he repeatedly exclaimed, "Truly, a divine spark dwells in this Schubert!" In short, the regard that Beethoven gained for Schubert's talent was so great that he now wished to see his operas and piano music; only the progression of his sickness at the time prevented him from fulfilling this wish. Yet he often spoke of Schubert and prophesied that he would yet create a stir in the world.

Anselm Hüttenbrenner reports of Beethoven's funeral:

> Schubert walked in the funeral procession carrying a burning candle. After the ceremony was finished, the friends found themselves together at the inn called "Auf der Mehlgrube" at the Neue Markt. "To him whom we have just buried!," Schubert proposed at the first toast. And for the second, "To him who will be next!"

The next was Franz Schubert himself. But he was not just the next one to follow Beethoven in death; he was also next in the sense that he was the greatest musical genius after Beethoven. When we consider how much more difficult it was to say great and valid things in music after Beethoven; moreover, when we think that Schubert in his short life of thirty-one years was not granted the chance to unfold his genius fully (as

Handel, Haydn, and Gluck were); and when we contemplate the mysterious depth and sublime height which Schubert reached in the Octet, in the B-flat Major Trio, in the Quartet Opus 161, and above all in the C Major Quintet, we do not hesitate to say that after the three uncontested kings of music—Bach, Mozart, and, the incomparable and unsurpassable Beethoven—perhaps Schubert's genius ranks next, for "truly, a divine spark dwells in this Schubert!"

Appendix

Additional Writings on Music

i. Sacred Music[1]

Sacred music represents its own kind of union between word and sound. We use this term as a designation not only of music that has a sacred ethos, like many of Bruckner's symphonies, but also of the music that is composed to sacred texts, for example, those of the mass or other parts of the liturgy, such as the Magnificat.

From the outset we must draw a clear distinction between oratorios that have no sacred character and the music set to sacred texts in its various forms. We limit ourselves to the latter. We shall discuss Gregorian chant, religious cantatas, Bach's *Christmas Oratorio* and *St. Matthew Passion*, Mozart's unfinished Mass in C Minor, and Beethoven's *Missa solemnis*.

These works contain a different relationship between music and word,

---

1. As published in Hildebrand's *Aesthetics*, vol. 2 (Steubenville, OH: Hildebrand Press, 2018), 503–10.

since the theme is no longer only artistic. It is above all a religious theme, something that belongs to the liturgy.

Gregorian chant and polyphonic church music. Thematic and unthematic beauty

Among all the masses that have been composed, those sung in Gregorian and Ambrosian chant occupy a unique position because they do not have an artistic theme of their own. The Holy Sacrifice of the mass is the theme, and the attitude of prayer permeates everything. The singing is primarily a solemn, elevated manner of speaking. The words have an absolute primacy as pure prayer, as the praise of God, and the singing participates fully in this prayer.

This kind of music is not in any way a representation or depiction but an expression, by the group of cantors and the choir, of the attitude of prayer. It varies in its connection with the words of the liturgy, according to the feast or liturgical season. Even someone who does not sing along is drawn into the spirit of the prayers. For both singers and nonsingers, the music of Gregorian chant is something enacted [*ein Vollzogenes*], that is, it does not address us as listeners, as even the most sublime and qualitatively loftiest sacred artistic music does. Rather, the singing of the Gregorian masses is completely united to the performance of the sacred rite. The only function of the sublime beauty of the chant is to give wings to our sharing in the enactment of the mystery of the Holy Sacrifice and of Holy Communion.

It is characteristic of this beauty to be unthematic.[2] Plato's dialogues are of great beauty, but the theme is not this beauty but truth, just as truth is thematic in St. Augustine's *Confessions*. Anyone who treated such works primarily as works of art would fail to do justice to them. He would misunderstand them profoundly. By contrast, even as great truths are uttered in Hamlet, its theme is the artistic beauty of the drama.

We have seen in an earlier chapter that the depth and degree of the

---

2. On this, see *Aesthetics*, vol. 1, chap. 13.

beauty of a work do not depend on whether its beauty is thematic. The great beauty of Gregorian chant does not alter the fact that it is not thematic but purely ancillary.

Polyphonic Masses

Something completely new is involved in polyphonic masses, in which only the fixed parts (the "Ordinary"), not the changing parts (the "Proper"), are set to music. Originally, they too were wholly at the service of the enactment of the sacred rite, but the music increasingly acquired a function of its own. Consider the masses that, from an artistic point of view, are greatest, Mozart's Mass in C Minor (K. 427)[3] and Beethoven's *Missa solemnis*. These polyphonic masses are much more extended than the masses composed in Gregorian chant. Each part represents in an unsurpassed manner the spirit of mystery, the greatness and holiness of what happens in the Holy Mass. But the music is no longer exclusively the praying of the liturgical words raised up in song. It is also itself an unsurpassed representation of the content of the individual words and indeed the mystery of the Holy Mass.

What fullness and heart-melting sweetness we find in the Christe eleison of Mozart's Mass in C Minor! What a representation of the beauty of the sacred humanity of Christ! How this music envelops us with the breath of mercy! How the glorious Et incarnatus est expresses the contemplative immersion in the tremendous mystery of the Incarnation! How we are touched by the breath of the ineffable sweetness of the Blessed Virgin! Obviously, something more is here than just an inspired, highly solemn enactment of the creed. Rather, the content of the words is represented through artistic means, in which certain parts of the text, when their meaning calls for it, take up a much larger space in the music than others.

This representation of the prayer's content in the music is a new element that clearly distinguishes these polyphonic masses from Gregorian

---

3. This judgment is not altered by the fact that parts of the Credo and the Agnus Dei are completed using other masses of Mozart.

chant. It is true that a polyphonic mass, too, is conceived for the act of worship; its music has only an ancillary function, and the theme remains the purely religious theme, the mystery of the Holy Mass. But the union of word and sound is new when compared with Gregorian chant.

The music unfolds its various expressive possibilities so as fully to express the religious text by way of artistic transposition. The believer is, so to speak, drawn through the music into the world of Christ. This sacred artistic beauty provides a new way to draw the souls of believers *in conspectum Dei* ("before the face of God") and to immerse them in the holy mystery of redemption. This is not antithetical to participating in the celebration of the sacred rite. Anyone who has experienced this Mozart mass in the liturgy will surely agree on the fully organic harmonization of one's inner participation in the celebration of the mass and one's being drawn into the sacred atmosphere through the artistic beauty of the music and through the musical representation of the religious content.

This does not alter the fact that Gregorian chant is the most appropriate music for the celebration of the Holy Mass. Already the fact that the sections of a polyphonic mass are much more time-consuming skews the proportions of the mass that enable inner participation.

Mozart's Mass in C Minor, which unfortunately remained unfinished, is in itself a great work of art that can be performed in the concert hall. This specifically sacred work of art appeals from the outset to an attitude completely different from *The Marriage of Figaro* or *The Magic Flute*.

This prompts the question: Is the beauty of this work thematic, or is it unthematic, even when performed in a concert?

This composition is an exceptional case, because Mozart did not intend it as a work of art, where artistic beauty is thematic and constitutes the *raison d'être*, but for the liturgy, the theme of which is the sacred celebration. It is, nevertheless, also a great, sacred work of art.

There can be no doubt that the artistic beauty is thematic in a concert, although in its quality this beauty is profoundly sacred and wholly united to the words of the Holy Mass. Even in the concert hall, one must never forget that this composition is meant for the mass. Above all, one should understand that the music employs artistic means to represent in an extremely intense manner the meaning of the liturgical texts and the world of the sacred. It gives glory to God through its spiritual quality, and it represents a form of prayer.

In the still more perfect polyphonic mass, namely, Beethoven's *Missa solemnis*, the representation of the mystery of the Holy Mass with artistic means is accomplished in a unique manner. The sacred seriousness that pervades everything, and the deep involvement with the text, above all with the meaningful content of the text, make it the polyphonic mass *par excellence*. This is why it is also an entry to the world of Christ, which could lead someone with a real artistic openness to conversion. The Sanctus draws us perfectly into the attitude of trembling reverence immediately prior to the consecration. The restraint and profoundly liturgical character of the music for the words "*Sanctus, sanctus, sanctus Dominus Deus Sabaoth*" is also the perfect expression of these words. What exultation in the Pleni sunt coeli! This music, so closely united to the word, unfolds its highest expressive possibilities. This is followed by the sublime Interlude. In the Benedictus after the consecration, the music reaches its high point, when through artistic means it represents the mystery of redemption, grace, and mercy. This Benedictus breathes in an incomparable manner the spirit of Christ the Redeemer. In it we find not just a perfect realization of the union of word and sound, but also of the penetration of the music by the nature and meaning of the Holy Mass.

The *Missa solemnis* likewise has an ancillary character. It fits wonderfully into the framework of the celebration of the mass. At the same time, it cannot be denied that it is above all in the concert hall that it unfolds its full artistic greatness and its deep sacrality. It is a work of art, but a sacred work of art. It is primarily an artistic representation—even *the* representation—of the spirit of the Holy Mass. Its sublime artistic beauty is fully thematic; but, on the other hand, it is so unambiguously sacred and so much a religious confession that one cannot do justice either to Beethoven's intention or to the spirit of the work if one listens to it as a pure work of art, that is to say, with the same attitude with which one listens to a symphony. Despite the thematic character of the artistic beauty, the theme of the whole remains purely religious.

Bach's St. Matthew Passion

A further kind of sacred music is Passion music. Bach's *St. Matthew Passion* is a work conceived for the liturgy. Its theme is clearly religious, namely, the Passion of the Lord. With regard to the union of word and sound, we must distinguish between music composed for the text of the Gospel; for the recitatives, arias, and choruses to a text by Picander (also known as Christian Friedrich Henrici) written for this *Passion*; and for the chorales, some of which have texts by Paul Gerhardt.

This music is completely formed by the spirit of the Gospel. The *St. Matthew Passion* is a high point of representation; indeed, it attains a unity with the spirit of the Passion of Christ that we can hardly still call "representation." When the Gospel is involved, the text is granted absolute primacy, whether in the music of the Evangelist or in the passages in which Jesus himself or another person speaks. But the passages of the Evangelist are not everywhere mere recitative, but sometimes attain a great expressive power through the pure beauty of the music, such as when the Evangelist repeats in German the words of Christ on the Cross, "*Eli, Eli, lama sabachthani!*" When Christ himself speaks, the music has sublime beauty and great expressive power simply *qua* music. When the crowd cries out, "Barabbam!" the full power of pure artistic expression is revealed to us. But in all this the word remains in the foreground. Sound and word interpenetrate, but the word has the leading role.

The situation in the *St. Matthew Passion* regarding the poems written by Bach's contemporaries is different. Here, the music has an absolute primacy. Its beauty and greatness rise far above the words. The music represents the world of the Gospel much more deeply and adequately than the text; it is united with the text in such a way that it draws it up far above its own value. The music has absolutely the leading role. The text serves the music to permit it to unfold the immeasurable wealth of its expression and to draw us fully into the world of the Gospel. In the chorales, with their liturgical character, music and word are equal in rank.

Here again the question arises: What is the theme of the *St. Matthew*

Passion, its beauty or the liturgical participation in the Passion of the Lord? Doubtless the latter is the theme and also Bach's intention.

At the same time, the *St. Matthew Passion* is also a consummate work of art. It appears—as in the case of the *Missa solemnis*—that the question of the theme is much more complicated. Even though the Gospel far surpasses in beauty everything else that has ever been written, its only theme is divine truth and revelation, not beauty. In the *Missa solemnis* and in the *St. Matthew Passion*, the answer is obviously not so clear. In their theme, they are fully at the service of the liturgy and the adoration of God. In their content, they fully represent the sacred. At the same time, both are great works of art, and as such beauty is thematic in both as well.

We need not investigate again the difference between the union of word and sound in these works and as it occurs in opera and music drama. Absent is the fashioning of a cast of characters, gone is the stage. But the comparison is instructive, since it shows us that artistic beauty is clearly the theme and *raison d'être* in opera and music drama. In a certain sense, the *Missa solemnis* and the *St. Matthew Passion* have two themes. The first is the theme intended by the artist, the purely religious theme. Both these works present a purely religious musical treatment of this sacred world. But since this representation presupposes a great artistic transposition, we have also the birth of a work of art in which by its nature beauty is thematic. Thus, there are two themes, each thematic in a different sense.

Bach's Christmas Oratorio *and cantatas*

Bach's *Christmas Oratorio* is clearly dedicated to the liturgy. Unlike the *St. Matthew Passion*, there are more arias and choruses than recitatives of the Evangelist. But this oratorio, too, is an example of the unique interpenetration of music and the representation of a mystery, in this case, the birth of Christ. The sinfonietta radiates with great intensity the world of the shepherds of Bethlehem on Christmas night. Words fail to express how powerfully this work represents the atmosphere of that grace-filled night of Bethlehem and of the entire Christmas season.

At the same time, the *Christmas Oratorio* is a great work of art, employing purely artistic means to immerse us into the mystery of the birth of Christ, even when performed in a concert hall. It is a representation of the sacred world and atmosphere of this supreme event, and an expression of the faith and the adoration of believers.

The twofold theme of the purely religious and liturgical, on the one hand, and of artistic beauty, on the other, can also be found in Bach's cantatas. In the context of the liturgy, they are fully at the service of the celebration of the religious ceremony. At the same time, they express the atmosphere of the feast and the theme of the texts. The artistic treatment of the religious content by the sacred beauty of the music makes them structures in which the beauty not only is a metaphysical beauty grounded entirely in other values but also bears the character of artistic beauty. We have here not just the metaphysical beauty of the religious content, nor just the metaphysical beauty of the religious content wonderfully expressed through artistic means, but also a purely artistic beauty of the music. Since beauty is thematic in the cantatas, they can be performed as works of art in the concert hall.

In addition to the masses of Mozart and Beethoven we have already mentioned, Bach's Mass in B Minor, Schubert's Mass in E-flat Major, the *Requiem* of Mozart and of Verdi, Bruckner's *Te Deum*, and his "Great" Mass in F Minor are significant works of art. If we think also of Bach's many cantatas or the sublime music of Mozart's Ave verum and Laudate Dominum, we see again how music in union with a sacred theme rises to the ultimate artistic heights.

Many dramatic expressive possibilities, such as fashioning characters in opera and music drama, do not exist in sacred music. In polyphonic masses, the texts have the absolute leading role, and the same is true of oratorios when the music is united to words of the Gospel. This does not apply to the texts in Bach's oratorios written by his contemporaries, and even less in his cantatas. Here the music has the leading role. The words are more of a basis on which the music can unfold its expressive possibilities. That which is represented is the object of which the words speak. But the form and the treatment of the object in the words is secondary in comparison with its representation in the music. In the glorious aria in Bach's cantata *Vergnügte Ruh', beliebte Seelenlust* (BWV 170), the music is entirely in the lead. It is incomparably more beautiful and profound than the text, which merely offers an occasion for what is sung. The music freely represents the religious content, without binding itself to the text.

ii. Beethoven's *Fidelio*[4]

The libretto of Beethoven's *Fidelio* is not a play that would be viable as a purely literary work. But it has a high moral content and a human depth that offer the music a unique possibility for development. It is exceedingly characteristic of Beethoven that he chose this hymn in praise of wedded love as the theme for his opera.[5] This libretto, which is less refined and dramatically formed than those of *Figaro* and *Don Giovanni*, has an enormous dramatic potency and provides the music a basis for a completely new expressive dimension. Particularly interesting is that the music "speaks" a completely different language and unfolds a different kind of dramatic art from that in Mozart. The characters are not fully fashioned dramatic figures, as in *Figaro* and *Don Giovanni*, though the character of Leonore is infused by the music with a greatness and depth that we do not find anywhere in Mozart. The injustice of the evil Pizarro, the sufferings of innocent captives, the benevolence and nobility of the Minister—all proclaim the ultimate significance of the moral sphere.

In *Fidelio* the metaphysical beauty of the moral sphere is expressed through the exclusively artistic means of music with a depth that is truly extraordinary. This also applies to Florestan and even to Fernando. What is more, there is also an intimate union between the pure beauty of the music and the metaphysical beauty of the moral world as we find it in

---

4. As published in Hildebrand's *Aesthetics*, vol. 2 (Steubenville, OH; Hildebrand Press, 2018), 470–75.

5. Gluck's *Alceste* is likewise a song of praise of heroic married love, but it lacks the sharp antithesis between good and evil. The breath of morality does not breathe through the whole work, as it does through *Fidelio*.

Leonore's profound love and fidelity and in Florestan's sufferings for the truth. Here we encounter a new style of dramatic art, a new language that touches our hearts to the core and moves us in a deeply personal way. What a voice of ultimate moral nobility we hear in the prisoners' chorus and in Florestan's recitative and aria in the second act.

In *Fidelio*, there is an incomparable interpenetration of text and music and the subject matter they share. The music treats the theme of the text with complete seriousness. The drama fashioned in this opera is of immense proportions. In it we find for the first time an articulated form of an inner or contemplative drama [*innerer oder Kontemplativer Dramatik*], which sharply distinguishes itself from outward drama [*äußeren Dramatik*]. In speaking of the "dramatic," one usually envisages, correctly, a suspenseful plot dynamically pressing forward, since this is an essential trait of the dramatic. But alongside this grand, dynamic form of drama, there is also a contemplative drama in which the suspense moves entirely to a deeper plane and the drama unfolds through intensity and depth. Consider for instance the scene in *King Lear* with the blinded Gloucester and Poor Tom (his son Edgar, whom he does not recognize), and also the nocturnal scene in Juliet's room in *Romeo and Juliet*.

In opera, we find an example of this contemplative drama in *Fidelio* in the duet, "O namen-namenlose Freude!" ("Oh inexpressible joy!"). This follows the scene, which is immensely dramatic in the dynamic sense, "Töt' erst sein Weib!" ("Kill first his wife!"), and the trumpet call—a moment of highest suspense conveyed indescribably by the music with this signal. The world "vanishes" in the loving gaze [*Ineinanderblick*] of Florestan and Leonore, in the contrast of their bliss and the terrible sufferings they have endured. This joy expresses itself in boundless jubilation, both in its inner dynamism and in the full contemplative expansion of bliss, in the passage, "O Gott, wie groß ist dein Erbarmen!" ("Oh God, how great is your mercy!"). We find the inner drama again in the wonderful passage "O Gott! O welch ein Augenblick!" ("Oh God, what a moment!") at the end of the opera.

Even though in the type of opera represented by *Fidelio* not all the characters are dramatically fashioned in the full Shakespearean sense as they are in *Figaro* and in *Don Giovanni*, nevertheless, *Fidelio* attains a high point all its own in the interpenetration of drama and music. The figures of Leonore and Florestan are not indeed figures in the Shakespearean sense, like the Countess, Susanna, and others in *Figaro*, but in another respect they are much more significant and profound than any character in Mozart. In their moral nobility, they are the soul of the entire dramatic progression. In the depth they manifest, they are representatives of a lofty moral world. This air of moral greatness is conveyed through purely musical means in a consummate artistic transposition.

A *secco* recitative would be utterly unsuited to the style of *Fidelio*. Only the spoken word could do justice to the style of the whole, to the extent that breaks between the music are even necessary. The transition from spoken to sung word makes for a tremendous impression in the first act, when Rocco says to Fidelio, "Meinst du, ich könnte dir nicht ins Herz sehen?" ("Do you think that I could not see into your heart?"), which is followed by the wonderful quartet "Mir ist so wunderbar" ("I feel so wonderful"). This organic transition and ascent from word to music has a particularly strong effect, in the best sense of the term. In union with the word, the music is able to express things for which the word alone would be inadequate.

We have already referred to the importance of the melodrama in the second act of *Fidelio*. The many fully formed *accompagnato* recitatives are sublime examples of this noble union of word and sound, this preparation for the unconstrained flow of the melody in the arias. We have in mind Leonore's recitative "Abscheulicher, wo eilst du hin?" ("Oh monster, where do you hasten to?") and, above all, Florestan's recitative in the second act, "Gott! Welch' Dunkel hier! O grauenvolle Stille!" ("God! How dark it is here! What terrible silence!").

Compared with Mozart's operas, the orchestra has a greater importance in *Fidelio*. It forms this drama extensively and therefore has a different relationship to what is sung from that in Mozart. The overture to *Fidelio* fulfills its dramatic function in a manner completely different from Mozart's overtures, which are themselves wonderful. Certainly, Mozart's overtures introduce us to the spirit of the opera, though not all to the same extent, the overture to *Figaro* least of all. The overture to *The Magic Flute* is less an introduction to the spirit of the opera than a significant piece of music in its own right.

The overture to *Fidelio* has a much more direct relationship to the drama. The full seriousness and the breath of moral greatness already sound in the overture and reveal the spirit of the opera as whole. The same is true of the orchestral interlude[6] at the beginning of the second act. The dramatic situation, the somber and eerie character of the dungeon, and the tragedy of Florestan, how remarkably all this is given! In these passages, the orchestra attains an unparalleled power of fashioning the drama.

We have already mentioned the power of music to fashion without words in the second act of *Orfeo ed Euridice*. The lyricism of this musical intermezzo is very meaningful for the world of Elysium. In *Fidelio*, on the other hand, the orchestra is fully integrated into the new way of shaping the drama. In every situation, in all the arias, including the duet between Rocco and Fidelio, "Nur hurtig fort" ("Make haste"), and especially in Florestan's reply, "O Dank dir!" ("Oh, thank you!"), the orchestra has been entrusted with an extremely important task in the construction and advancing of the drama. This has often been interpreted erroneously. The assertion that "Beethoven was not a dramatist like Mozart" is completely incorrect. It is true that Beethoven did not possess the specific dramatic gift that enabled Mozart to use musical means to thoroughly fashion his characters in Shakespearean manner. But Beethoven created a completely new dramatic dimension, which includes giving the orchestra a much larger task in the construction of the drama. This dramatic dimension is the bearer of a high artistic value and connected to a new form of the interpenetration of sound and word. Let us not forget that Beethoven felt himself compelled in what may be his greatest work, the Ninth Symphony, to introduce in the last movement a union of music and word that is a unique example of their interpenetration and the new concrete expressive possibilities that arise through this union. This by no means entails only the inclusion of human voices and the expression

---

6. [Hildebrand has in mind Beethoven's *Leonore* Overture No. 3, which is sometimes performed within the second act of *Fidelio*.—Trans.]

they possess in contrast to all instruments, but also the union of sound and word.

The conclusions to various operas is a further help in delineating the type of opera that *Fidelio* represents and the function of the music in the construction of the drama. The ending in *Figaro*, *Don Giovanni*, *Così fan tutte*, and also in *The Magic Flute*, is a return to a state of tranquility, a stylized fading away of the whole. In *Figaro*, the sublime and profound "Contessa, perdono!" ("Countess, your pardon!") is followed by a charming and cheerful roundelay. In *The Magic Flute*, after the glorious "Die Strahlen der Sonne vertreiben die Nacht" ("The rays of the sun drive away the night") there is likewise a kind of stylized fading away. These endings perfectly fit the framework of the stage to which Mozart adhered in a special way. In *Don Giovanni*, the grand scene with the Commendatore and the terrible downfall of Don Giovanni is followed by the wonderful, serene conclusion, which incorporates the world of human life in its full reality, with its radiant poetry. This ending strikes us as even more beautiful than those of *Figaro* and *The Magic Flute*. It restores the bright light of day in a brilliant manner, brings all the characters back on stage one last time, and wonderfully depicts how life goes on. Given the context of the stage, which entails a certain distance from the onlooker, this is a profoundly fitting conclusion. It is only in *Die Entführung*, which is closely related to the *Fidelio* type in many ways, that the conclusion, "Wer so viel Huld vergessen kann" ("Whoever can forget such grace"), in keeping with the ethos of the whole, is less of a fading away and a return to the framework of the stage. The conclusion to *Fidelio*, on the other hand, is something completely new. It is a high point. The apotheosis of marital fidelity shatters the framework of the stage. It is not a fading away but a victorious and glorious final resounding of the profoundly moral ethos that fills this entire work.

From a dramatic perspective, the role entrusted to the orchestra in Fidelio certainly justifies the insertion of the great *Leonore* Overture No. 3 following the duet "O namenlose Freude!" ("Oh inexpressible joy!"), a practice begun by Gustav Mahler.[7] "Justifies" strikes us as too weak, since

---

7. [This practice may have predated Mahler.—Trans.]

this insertion in fact is a particularly beautiful complement. Following the high dramatic suspense of the events on stage and the profound ensuing inner drama, the contemplative rhythm already present here comes to full expression with this insertion, which presents the figure of Leonore with purely musical means. Since the music of this overture is completely filled with the spirit of Leonore, it makes for a wonderful insertion that leads us to immerse ourselves contemplatively in this character and immerse ourselves in her spirit.

iii. Richard Wagner's music dramas[8]

In Wagner's music dramas we find a new kind of interpenetration of word and music, one that enables completely new expressive dimensions in music and is involved to such an extent in the construction of the drama that it is no longer possible to detach the music from the words. The plot does not present a skeleton that the music brings to life. Rather, the drama is constructed by word and music acting in complete unity, despite the fact that the music is artistically on a much higher level than the poetry.

This unification of music and word is aided to an extraordinary degree by the fact that the author is creator of both the music and the poetry. Each music drama in its totality is the invention of the artist. The words are never conceived independently of the music, nor the music independently of the words.

The unity of music and word already exists in the first sketch, in the fledgling desire to create something, in the initial vague conception, in the idea of a tale that Wagner is drawn to shape dramatically. Wagner is never inspired by an existing drama to compose the music and create an opera. The saga of the Flying Dutchman, for example, inspires him for the creation of this music drama. Although Wagner conceives the poem before he composes the music, every word is conceived in view of the music drama as a totality. Of course, this totality becomes ever more

---

8. As published in Hildebrand's *Aesthetics*, vol. 2 (Steubenville, OH; Hildebrand Press, 2018), 485–89.

music alone lacks and that presupposes the union of music and drama. Wagner achieves the ultimate interpenetration of music and drama in his greatest work, *Tristan und Isolde*, a work standing apart from all others by unfathomable depths, in which the unique inner drama fully unfolds in a contemplative manner.

The leitmotif has often been entirely misunderstood. It has been regarded as an abstract link between a musical theme and a meaningful content, as something externally imposed on the poetic text, making the music, at best, a mosaic of leitmotifs. This is totally inaccurate. In reality, there is nothing abstract about the link between a musical theme and a meaningful content, be it a person's fate, a given character's love, redemption and passion, or a phenomenon in nature. The element being represented is given in an immediate, intuitive expression that fulfills its dramatic function. Anyone with a true sensitivity for music and the union of word and music, for the interpenetration of music and drama and the new expressive possibilities of music revealed here, will be immersed in the contents of these elements when hearing and being affected by the music drama, even without knowing the names of these elements.

The leitmotif is in no way imposed on the poetic text from the outside. It has no illustrative function. It grows organically out of the dramatic inspiration. This does not make the music drama a mosaic of leitmotifs. Rather, these themes are entirely integrated into the music's inner logic as its flows on organically, and, thanks to the marriage of music and drama, they attach themselves to the subject matter of the poetic text, without disturbing the music's inner logic. In *The Flying Dutchman*, for example, the entire drama is structured through the leitmotifs of the Dutchman, the world of the sailors, and redemption.

Although themes outweigh typical melodies in Wagner's music drama, this does not at all mean that Wagner does not also use melodies for the construction of the drama as a whole. Walther's various songs and the glorious chorus in *Die Meistersinger*, "Wach auf, es nahet gen den Tag" ("Wake up, the day is near") as well as Lohengrin's song in the last act of the eponymous opera, when he reveals his identity, are definitely melodies, as are many other passages.

We must especially emphasize that countless themes that function as leitmotifs can be combined to form a great melody simply by dint of their musical quality, as happens in *Tristan* in a wonderful way in the "Liebestod."

iv. Selections from the unpublished essay on Richard Wagner[9]

On approaching the music of Wagner[10]

Wagner's works, particularly from *Rheingold* onward, demand a deep commitment on the part of the listener. Their beauty and greatness will remain hidden except to the person who approaches them in a spirit of complete openness and surrender and with a readiness to receive with great seriousness all that they have to offer.

This raises an important distinction concerning the unique character of a work of art and also concerning the attitude of the person addressed by the work. I already alluded to the difference between someone who goes to the theater to be amused and entertained and someone who wants to be moved and edified by a drama. But that is only a poor analogy for what I have in mind here. Music was often composed to serve as the background for a particular situation, such as a divertimento to be played during a meal; often music had a quasi-decorative function for a celebration. In like manner, many operas are simultaneously entertaining and beautiful, indeed full of great depth. Just as great and significant truths can be conveyed in lighter settings, in aphorisms, so great and profound beauty can appear in a form that does not from the outset require of the listener a spirit of *sursum corda*, recollection, and commitment.

But this calls for a further important distinction. On the one hand, there are works of art that do not call for this commitment and whose artistic content is of a more modest nature, while still possessing a definite artistic value, even if they fall short of great depth and sublimity. Rossini's charming *Barber of Seville* or Goldoni's little masterpiece *La*

---

9. Originally published in *St. Austin Review* (July/August 2017). 4–8. See the Note on the Text for additional information.

10. [Manuscript marked: 157/4 Seite f/p. F.]

locandiera fall into this category. Entertainment and artistic charm and gracefulness are masterfully fused in these works. On the other hand, there are also works of art where the element of entertainment is bound up with the highest expressions of artistic beauty and depth, as is the case with Mozart. This is what Walter Braunfels had in mind in one of his essays where he speaks of the special aesthetic value at hand when the deepest content is presented in the "lightest vessel."

An entirely different case involves noble and significant music that cannot move and uplift us like that of Mozart but the perfection and significance of which can inspire us, such as the First or Fourth Symphonies of Brahms. Here we find neither the "light vessel" nor the ultimate, highest beauty but a type of art that does not require our self-surrender, our *sursum corda*, in order to disclose its beauty, an art that calls for appreciation, joy, enthusiasm without rising to the level of a work that stirs, transfixes, or speaks to our deepest humanity. Many noble works of art fall into this category.

The case of Bach is again completely different. Here we encounter depth, sublime beauty, and perfection of the highest order. The note of entertainment is completely absent. We can do justice to a work only if we allow ourselves to be fully engaged, to move to a deeper level, and often to exert ourselves. But with Bach the appeal to the listener is quite different from that of Beethoven and Wagner. Bach's music asks us to enter in and to open ourselves, but the beauty does not remain hidden if we do not give ourselves over in a special way, nor does the music confront us with such a demand. It simply stands before us in its majestic and moving greatness—in a certain respect the greatest possible antithesis to entertainment.

It is not easy to express the special form of participation and self-surrender that we find in Beethoven and in an even more pronounced way in Wagner and also in Bruckner. All great and profound art in every domain, as well as the sublime beauty of nature, calls for a reverent self-surrender. It appeals to our deepest center and will not reveal itself if we shy away from depth and wish to remain on a superficial plane. But what I want to draw attention to in Wagner goes far beyond the call of all great beauty in nature and art.

Already Beethoven's music contains a very particular sort of appeal to the listener, in which we also find an ethical dimension. He bears witness and awakens us; indeed, he wants to awaken us. He addresses us in a special way, and his work calls us not just to respond with enthusiasm, recognition, appreciation, delight, and great enjoyment, but also to be alert, recollected, and deeply moved to the core of our humanity. To approach any of Beethoven's works with the attitude of the aesthete is totally contrary to his spirit. It is true that there are many people who greatly appreciate some of Beethoven's works, such as his late quartets, for their extraordinary perfection. They fail, however, to understand their real beauty. This can surely be said of all great and profound beauty, that it will not disclose itself to the aesthete with his severely self-absorbed attitude. But here it is a matter of recognizing that Beethoven's work requires a readiness to enter into the music that could not be more contrary to this self-absorbed aestheticism and that prohibits even the slightest commingling with aestheticism. Despite working with purely artistic materials like no one else, the music of this supreme artist so deeply embodies the ultimate mysterious connection of beauty and the world of moral values that it reaches us in the depth of our humanity. His inscription above the *Missa solemnis*, "From the heart: may it go to the heart" ("Vom Herzen, möge es wieder, zu Herzen gehen!"), express in words what his work requires of the listener.

Beginning with *Rheingold*, Wagner's works make demands on the listener that point in yet another direction. They share with Beethoven an ultimate seriousness toward the values they embody, which call us to a greater depth of existence and which stand in opposition both to mere entertainment and also to aestheticism. But Wagner demands a special form of commitment and self-surrender. Already the length of his works means that the listener must subordinate himself, put aside the theme of entertainment, and be fully given over to the work. Wagner's operas cannot be realized within the scope of the conventional theater; indeed, the founding of the festival in Bayreuth is a manifestation of the seriousness and total commitment they require.

Many people consider the demanding character of Wagner's music as arrogant and as something of an imposition. Others wish neither to dwell at a deeper level nor to do so in the measure needed. It is hardly surprising that such people dislike Wagner or, better said, that they are incapable of perceiving the greatness, beauty, and profundity of Wagner's work. The person who approaches a work like *Tristan* in this attitude is necessarily deaf and blind, insensitive to the mysterious depth and fascinating beauty of this "solitary work." We must be prepared to give ourselves to the work fully. If we do so, the reward is immense and incomparable.

Great Wagnerian inventions

It is impossible to do justice to Wagner without recognizing that he is above all a great dramatist. Now, I do not mean that he is primarily a poet. Quite the contrary, he is a musician through and through. But he is the creator of great dramas, realized primarily by means of music. They are music dramas [*Musikdramen*] and we cannot do justice to Wagner if we prescind from his invention of the drama, the characters, the dramatic situations, and the meaning and content of the word. Even less can we take the text alone and separate it from the music. For they form an inseparable unity, and even if a purely poetic formulation is not entirely satisfactory, it in no way reduces the greatness, depth, classical character of the drama, which precisely is realized primarily through the music. This must be affirmed—even if in so many passages the music itself is of ultimate beauty. But Wagner in his totality does not emerge in all his greatness until one sees him as a dramatist and until one sees the breathtaking beauty of the music in its power to shape the dramatic situation....[11]

Having called attention to Wagner's singular invention of a new artistic format, the music drama, let me now highlight certain foundational elements that come to unique expression in his works.[12]

I begin with Wagner's representations of the natural world, which I

---

11. [Manuscript, 7.]
12. [Manuscript, 9.]

mention first, not because they are of primary importance but because they represent something specifically new in the connection between drama and music. Of course, we find in Beethoven's Pastoral Symphony a wonderful representation of natural elements, while many of Schubert's songs capture the poetry of the great primordial phenomena of nature. But in Wagner the representation of the very "soul" of certain primordial phenomena—of water, blossoming in nature, the special poetry of the forest, light and shadow, the solitude and grandeur of mountain crag, fire, ocean and innumerable similar entities—attains a degree of embodiment in the music wherein the musical "representation" is naturally and closely woven into the drama itself. By providing the background, becoming embodied in certain figures, and shaping the dramatic situation, these natural elements play a relevant role in the drama. The manner in which the quality of these primordial phenomena is embodied by the music—in all of their particular character and poetry, greatness and mystery—is simply extraordinary. It is crucial to understand that the embodiment of these primordial phenomena differs radically from a merely imitative representation. The music in no way seeks to be illustrative; its purpose is not the musical imitation of natural occurrences. Rather, the spiritual quality of all these great natural phenomena and their inexhaustible qualitative richness is embodied in a way that bears a certain analogy to poetry....

Wagner is above all the great bard of love. He has brought to incomparable artistic expression this most primordial of all phenomena in all its most varying aspects. Indeed, this primordial phenomenon is so multidimensional that certain aspects of love find their highest expression in Mozart. It is not without reason that Wagner called Mozart the genius of light and love, and that Mozart, in commenting on the demands of musical genius, says that "love, love" is what is required above all. In Beethoven's *Fidelio* a completely different dimension of love, namely, heroic love, finds its highest embodiment—a dimension nowhere developed in Mozart. But in Wagner we find the matchless expression of a whole range of further dimensions of love. With *Tristan und Isolde*, Wagner created the drama of love *par excellence*, the tragedy not just of two lovers but of love here on earth, of human love. No one has penetrated this primordial phenomenon so deeply. No other work takes love so seriously and presents it in its ultimate intensity, in its ecstatic and metaphysical depth. Without doubt, Wagner surpasses all others as the bard of love.[13]

Another foundational theme that pervades Wagner's work is the antithesis between good and evil. Of course, as the axis of the spiritual world, of life and of all literature, this antithesis is the basis of every drama, be it *King Lear*, *Hamlet*, *Macbeth*, or *Othello*. Indeed, it is the presupposition for everything. And yet what I want to highlight here is the special role—the special thematic role—of this primordial phenomenon in Wagner's music dramas. Whether we consider *Tannhäuser* or *Lohengrin*, or look to the *Ring*, which embodies the incompatibility of pride and love, and naturally in a very particular way to *Parsifal*, without fail we encounter the particular drama of this primordial antithesis. The moral sphere has been fully transposed into an aesthetic dimension, without the slightest trace of any pedagogical purpose extrinsic to the work of art. No, what is thematic is the primordial drama of the antithesis between good and evil.[14]

Even more particular to and characteristic of Wagner is how deeply he grasps the phenomenon of redemption, and redemption in the Christian sense. This primordial phenomenon, for which so many Catholics today have lost any understanding, is so deeply grasped by Wagner and so uniquely presented in word and music—is given artistic expression in a way that is more convincing, moving, and poignant than in the work of any other great artist.[15]

Tannhäuser[16]

Hardly any dramatic work could have a more powerful subject than that of *Tannhäuser*. We find here the contrast of sin and holiness and the drama of Christian redemption—where intercession plays a decisive role.

13. [Manuscript, 10–11.]
14. [Manuscript, 11.]
15. [Manuscript, 11.]
16. [Manuscript, 21–23.]

The drama is totally immersed in the medieval world and filled with the air of penance, atonement, grace, and the mercy of God....

Tannhäuser's yearning to leave the Venusberg and to return to the real world is initially manifested in his desire to come back into contact with the purity of nature. He begins by perceiving the particular nobility and innocence of nature, the birdsong, the seasons, and the sound of bells calling him to truthfulness and awakeness. This is followed by the intolerable sense of being trapped in a purely immanent realm of conscience.

Tannhäuser marks the first time dramatic literature presents the impossibility of fulfilling the human soul with what is merely satisfying, pleasurable, and comfortable; and at the same time the ordination of the soul toward the world of objective values, toward what is important in itself. Basically it is an expression of the Augustinian *Fecisti nos ad te, Domine...* ("You have made us for yourself, O Lord, and our heart is restless until it rests in you"). This struggle, which represents the fundamental theme of earthly human existence—the temptation, on the one hand, to live only for what is pleasurable and satisfying and the weakness that leads us to do what we recognize to be unjust, and the reality, on the other hand, that the true happiness for which our deepest soul longs can be found only in our commitment to God and to objective values; the transcendence of the person and the prison of desire for that which is merely pleasurable—all of this *Tannhäuser* for the first time treats in dramatic fashion. Tannhäuser's words, "I crave pain," lends the oppressive quality of pure immanence a paradoxical expression. His yearning for the supernatural world, the ultimate antithesis to the Venusberg, finally breaks through to the realm of true transcendence, which is possible only through the redemption.

This brings us to one of the most beautiful and moving dramatic effects in the opera. The moment Tannhäuser utters the words "My salvation lies in Mary!"—expressing his yearning for salvation and for God through the Blessed Virgin—the Venusberg is undone. Mary embodies such ineffable purity that the specter of wicked lust and sin vanishes, flees, even just at the sound of her name. What a unique, wonderful dramatic inspiration! Then comes the scene of which Wilhelm Furtwängler has written so wonderfully. As soon as Tannhäuser has called upon the name of the Holy Virgin, he finds himself in a countryside filled with the air of springtime and morning. The great purity and clarity of unblemished nature stands before him and also before us....

Another great dramatic inspiration occurs with the appearance of the pure and noble Elisabeth, who ardently loves Tannhäuser, and with their encounter. Elisabeth embodies true spousal love, with its very particular ardor in which we find a completely pure, noble sensuality transfigured by love and reverence.... How grand is the horror that grips everyone at the mention of the Venusberg and at the fact that Tannhäuser dwelled there. Once again music and word express a primordial phenomenon, namely, the abyss that separates the Venusberg from the realm of holiness, the redemption, and the world of Christ—no, not just separates but presents in their ultimate antithesis....

Tristan und Isolde[17]

We come now to a work that occupies a unique place among the music dramas of Wagner. Indeed, this work is in every respect unique. A "word" is spoken here for which there is no analogue, whether in the realm of drama or in opera. It is a solitary work, about the drama of love as such. The primordial question expressed in the unique theme with which the Prelude begins—which embodies all of the longing of man and the entire tragedy of the human situation upon earth, and which is then answered in the extraordinary and ineffable love-theme—leads us into an ultimate depth and profoundly stirring spiritual solitude.

All other great dramas about love, *Romeo and Juliet*, for example, speak of a tragic fate that befalls the lovers. Yet here we have to do with the tragedy of love as such, the impossibility of fulfilling the desire of the ultimate *intentio unionis* [desire for union with the beloved] while on earth, the tension between life in its everyday dryness and the ultimate ecstatic awakedness. This tragedy is a reflection of the tension between the ultimate ecstatic love for Jesus and the earthly circumstances that

17. [Manuscript, 1–2.]

press us from one concern to another. Of course, it is objectively only a reflection, and Wagner in this work does not call attention to the fact that it is but a reflection. Yet in the music, especially that in the *Liebestod* in the second and third acts, there dwells a beatitude far surpassing the love of man and woman—even in all of its metaphysical depth—and reflecting the beatitude of the mystic's ecstatic love for Jesus.

The music of *Tristan* lacks any sacred character. In *Tannhäuser*, *Lohengrin*, and above all in *Parsifal*, the music in many respects has a definitely sacred character. The Benedictus in the *Missa solemnis* of Beethoven or the *St. Matthew Passion* of Bach reach the pinnacle of the sacred. It is not a sacred note in the music of the *Liebestod* that justifies our saying that it reflects the love of the holy mystics—of a St. Catherine of Siena or a St. Teresa of Avila. The unique ardor, depth, ecstasy, and beatitude of love is wonderfully expressed in the Song of Songs, which is constantly used as an analogy in the liturgy for the love between the soul and Jesus, particularly in the mass texts for feasts of the Blessed Virgin. The Song of Songs is also used as an analogy for the mystical union of love with Christ in the indescribable poem of St. John of the Cross.[18] In *Tristan*, as in the Song of Songs, it is the depth, ardor, and beatitude of this highest expression in music of the deepest human love that make certain passages an expression of the love of the holy mystics.

In *Tristan*, the genius of Wagner enables the great artist to surpass his personal worldview—like Goethe at the end of the first part of *Faust*. The phenomenon of redemption, and redemption in Christ, which found such wonderful expression in *Tannhäuser* and *Parsifal*, is not what occupies Wagner in *Tristan*. The words in *Tristan* in many places contain a note of Schopenhauer's philosophy, which at the time had made a deep impression on Wagner. But this note in no way prevents the entire work from being the greatest, deepest classical expression of spousal love, indeed, by expressing spousal love in its spiritual essence and liberated from all earthly tragedy, from becoming an expression of the love of the mystics to Jesus and through Him to God. The music expresses an ulti-

---

18. [Hildebrand most likely has in mind the *Spiritual Canticle*.—Trans.]

mate beatitude—which objectively is possible only through unification with Jesus.

v. Verdi's music dramas *Otello* and *Falstaff*[19]

We conclude our analysis of the music drama with a reference to Verdi's two masterpieces, *Otello* and *Falstaff*. It is a unique occurrence in the history of opera that a master, after a life of great productivity, suddenly ascends at the age of seventy to an act of artistic creation far surpassing all his earlier works, both in the union of music and drama and in its purely musical quality. Already in his *Requiem* we find a spirit that surpasses everything he had previously created. Verdi's earlier works contain many passages of musical beauty and are full of ideas of a dramatic kind, but the *Requiem* in its depth and sublime artistic beauty cannot be compared to what preceded it.

In *Otello* and *Falstaff*, Verdi created two music dramas of a high dramatic creative power, a completely original type of the interpenetration of music and drama, different from that in Wagner. Of course, one cannot overlook the formal influence of Wagner in many regards. Both these music dramas are through-composed, without the arias so typical of the earlier Verdi. The orchestra has a much greater importance, and the leitmotif, too, is present to a certain extent.

These music dramas, as is generally known, derive from Shakespeare. The mighty tragedy *Othello* is such a consummate masterpiece in its own right that its performance never leads one to think of a possible union with music. Shakespeare's play is of such perfection and greatness that one cannot say the music of Verdi's *Otello* heightens its artistic value.

Nevertheless, this music drama is a masterpiece. The existence of Verdi's music drama in addition to Shakespeare's play means a great enrichment for art.

This brings us the general question, namely, which dramas, plays, and comedies are even suitable to be united with music. We are thinking only

---

19. As published in Hildebrand's *Aesthetics*, vol. 2 (Steubenville, OH; Hildebrand Press, 2018), 493–95.

of works that stand on their own [*eigenständige Werke*], that are not just viable but also possess a high artistic value. This question does not arise with Wagner, not just because poetry and music derive from the same author, but because they are conceived from the very outset in view of their union and mutually complement each other. This question also does not obtain for mere librettos that are unviable in themselves.

It is very striking that the texts of Shakespeare's *Othello* and Verdi's music drama are not identical. Boito altered Shakespeare's work in certain places and made it suitable for a music drama. The first act in Venice, which is very important for the play, is omitted. Secondly, the figure of Iago is somewhat modified through the insertion of the diabolical "credo." In Shakespeare, Iago is an incarnation of villainy and moral baseness. In the music drama, he becomes a fundamental representative of evil and acquires a kind of diabolical greatness. Finally, the insertion of Desdemona's "Ave Maria," a musical high point, is indeed profoundly in keeping with the Shakespearean character, but it is nevertheless an alteration.

This means that certain alterations are essential in order for achieving the interpenetration of music and drama and for the perfection and effect of the music drama. Boito displayed great artistic wisdom here. As the creator of *Mefistofele*, he was himself not an unimportant operatic composer.

In Verdi's *Otello*, we find an intense interpenetration of music and poetry, for example, in the second act, when Iago describes the dream of Cassio that he claims to have overheard. This is a passage of supreme musical-dramatic power. How unsurpassably the music captures the character of the dream. How expressively it fashions Iago, how incomparably it expresses the alleged love of Cassio for Desdemona. How it expresses the insubstantial and ultimately evanescent character of the dream. This is preceded by Othello's deeply moving song "Della gloria d'Otello è questo il fin!" ("This is the end of Othello's glory!"). How powerful when he swears his revenge at the end of the second act!

There is a completely different relationship between poetry and music in Verdi's *Falstaff*. Shakespeare's comedy *The Merry Wives of Windsor* stands fully on its own, and Boito's plot sticks closely to it. But the music drama *Falstaff* is a far greater work of art than Shakespeare's comedy. The figure of Falstaff, a magnificent artistic creation in *Henry IV*, is presented even more fully and potently by the music than in *The Merry Wives*. The second act, with Mistress Ford, Falstaff, the return of Master Ford, and Fenton's visit, has music of extraordinary power in purely musical and also dramatic terms. The music is also highly poetic in the theme of the love between Fenton and Nannetta.

In the chapters about opera and music drama, we emphasized the great artistic possibilities for development attained by music through its union with drama. This form of the work of art cannot create any higher artistic values than absolute music and pure drama, but it can realize other values that neither music nor drama is capable of giving on its own. And these values are just as high as those of absolute music and of drama.

Index

Aestheticism, 32, 88
Artistic beauty, 70, 73, 75–76, 87
    Thematic and unthematic beauty, 70–75
    Metaphysical beauty, 76–77
Antipersonalism, 2, 26

Beauty, concept of, 2, 18, 23, 35, 70, 75, 86–89
    Sublime beauty, 13, 15, 66, 70, 74, 87

Classical (in Hildebrand's sense of the term) 2, 7, 16, 28, 33, 46, 48, 89, 95
    Classical hierarchy, 24, 39
    Classical humor, 8, 12, 15
    Classicity, 2, 28
    Classical (era), 48, 62
        Contrast with Romanticism, 24–25, 48, 62
Commitment, 86–89
Confessional character [*Bekenntnis*], 37–38
Coincidentia oppositorum, 3, 38, 46, 48
Contemplative, 39–40, 55, 61, 63–64, 71, 78, 82, 85

Drama in music, 5–13, 36, 59, 76–81, 83–97
    Contemplative drama, 78, 82, 85
    Inner drama, 36, 78, 82–85
Duality in artistic expression, 3, 46
    Darkness and light, 22, 39
    Entertainment and high artistic expression, 87–88
    Joy and sorrow, 33–34, 45–46
    Tension and tranquility, 39
    Tragedy and joy, 33, 39, 45–46

Entertainment, 13, 87–88
Ethos, 2, 5, 7–8, 15, 21, 27–28, 31–34, 69
    Catholic ethos, 20–21
    Moral ethos, 7, 15, 81

Form, 17–18, 25–26, 27–29, 32, 33, 35, 39–40
    Ecstasy of form, 40
    Looser form, 25, 48, 58
    Taut form, 33, 46, 58
Freedom, 4, 6, 14–16, 29, 39–40, 58
Freemasonry, 20

Genius, xx, 1–4, 20, 23, 28, 31, 43–45, 54, 60, 64, 66, 67–68
    Genius of Austria, 21, 44
Gospels, 21, 74–76

Humor, 3, 5, 7–8, 12, 15, 19, 36

Inner law, 26, 29, 40
Inner necessity [*innere Notwendigkeit*], 2, 4, 12, 17, 29, 30, 40

Joy, 3, 8, 9, 11, 18, 19, 22, 26, 27, 33–34, 39, 42, 45–46, 64–65, 78, 87

Kitsch, 2

Leitmotif, 11, 83–86, 95
Liturgy, 19, 37, 69–76, 94
    Holy Mass, 42, 70–73
    Liturgical participation, 72
    Liturgical or sacred texts, 69–73
Love, xx, 4, 11, 13, 16, 26–27, 34, 36–37, 58, 62, 78, 90–94
    Ecstatic love, 93–94
    Heroic love, 77, 90
    Human love, 91, 94
    Mystical union, 94–95
    Spousal love, 34, 93, 95

Melancholy, xx, 45, 55
Moral dimension in music, 5, 7, 10–11, 15, 77–79, 81, 88, 91
    Antithesis between good and evil, 77, 91
    Moral ethos, 7, 15, 81
    Moral nobility, 11, 78–79
Music and poetry, 53–59, 69, 73–75, 78–79, 82–85, 96
    Enhancement of the poem, 53–54
    Interpenetration of word and music, 59, 74, 78–80, 82–83
Music critic, xxiv, 2–3

Music drama, 17, 54, 75–76, 82–85, 89, 91, 93, 95–97
Mystery, xx, 2, 21, 29, 39, 40, 61–62, 71–73, 75, 90

Nature, 4, 22, 24, 32–34, 48, 85, 87, 90, 92–93
    Beauty of nature, 57, 87
    Naturwelten, 34, 38, 84
    Representation in music, 34, 48, 55–57, 62, 66, 84, 90, 92–93
Negative qualities in music
    Arbitrariness, 24, 27–28
    Cheapness, 18, 25, 38,
    Kitsch, 2
    Superficiality, 9, 18, 87
    Triviality, 2, 47
    Ugliness, 18
New functionalism, 2, 26

Objectivity, 2, 24, 26–28, 32, 37, 92
    Contrasted with neutrality, 26
    Objective logos, 27–28
    Subjectivity vs. objectivity, 24, 26–27, 38
    Values and, 24, 32–33, 92
Opera, 4–17, 36–37, 59, 77–97
    Role of the orchestra, 79–82, 83–84. 95
    Through-composition, 83–84, 95

Primordial, 12, 31, 38, 57
    Primordial phenomena
        Love, 90–91
        Nature, 90
        Redemption, 91

Redemption, 21, 42, 72–73, 85, 91–94
Recollection, 41, 47, 63, 86
Relativism, 1–2, 20
Reverence, 18, 34, 73, 87, 93
Romanticism, 2, 24–26, 30, 32, 48, 50–51
    Contrast with Classicism, 24–26, 48

INDEX

Sacred music, 69–76
   Co-presence of religious and artistic themes, 74–76
   Gregorian chant, 69–72
   Masses, 20–21, 34, 38, 40, 42, 61, 69–76, 88, 94
      Polyphonic masses, 71–73, 76
   Oratorios, 69, 75–76
   Passion music, 20, 69, 74–75, 94
   Religious cantatas, 69, 75–77
   Sacred texts, 69, 71–74, 76–77
Seriousness, 11, 20, 23, 30–32, 37–38, 41, 50, 78, 80, 86, 88
Spirituality in music, 3–4, 17, 31–32, 40–41, 47, 69–76

Subjectivity, 2, 24, 26–27, 38
   Contrast with objectivity, 24, 26–27
   Self-indulgence, 27–28, 32, 41
Sublime, 6, 13, 15, 31, 35–36, 39–40, 46–47, 51, 64, 68, 81
Surrender, 27, 86–89

Theme (musical), 31–32, 63–64, 83, 84–86
Tragic/tragedy
   Joy and, 11, 39, 18–19, 46
   Tragedy of world and mankind, 19, 42, 45, 93

Uncanny, 47, 49, 55, 58, 63, 83

Value-response, 26–28, 32, 34, 41–42

Index of Names

Augustine, St., 30, 70, 92

Bach, Johann Sebastian, 2, 20, 23, 39–40, 47, 68, 75, 77, 87
    Comparison with other composers, 39, 44, 47, 68–69
Beaumarchais, Pierre-Augustin Caron de, 7
Beethoven, Ludwig van, 1–2, 12, 21, 23–42, 43–44, 48, 51–53, 59, 61, 64–65, 67–68, 71, 73, 76–81, 87–88, 90, 94, 99
    Artistic characteristics
        Antithesis to tragic, 33–34
        Ethos, 26–28, 31–34
        Freedom and depth, 29, 39–40
        Form, 26–29, 32–33, 35, 39–40, 46
        Joy, 33–34, 39, 42
        Objectivity, 2, 26–28, 37
        Seriousness, 37–38, 88
        Universality, 35–36
    Comparison with Mozart, 37–38,
    Heiligenstadt Testament, 32
    Influence on Schubert, 43, 51–52, 67
    Mission to humanity, 40–42
    Misunderstanding of, 24–25, 32–34
    Romanticism and, 24–25, 30, 32
    Sacred music, 35, 37–38, 42, 73
Berlioz, Hector, 24, 44
Boito, Arrigo, 96, 97
Brahms, Johannes, 24, 44, 87
Braunfels, Walter, 1, 19–20, 87
Brueghel, Pieter, 2
Bruckner, Anton, 23, 44, 69, 76, 87

Catherine of Siena, St., 94
Cervantes, Miguel de, 10
Chopin, Frédéric, 1, 24–25
Claudius, Matthias, 55

Danhauser, Josef, 50
Dante, 23

Eichendorff, Joseph von, 24, 25, 46
Eugene of Savoy, 21

Fra Angelico, 23
Furtwängler, Wilhelm, 9n, 25–26, 28, 29, 32, 39, 53, 55, 93

INDEX OF NAMES

Giorgione, 62
Gluck, Christoph Willibald, 4–5, 17, 39, 47, 51, 53, 68, 77, 80
Goethe, Johann Wolfgang von, 1, 14, 24, 59
    Faust, 55, 94
    poems set to music by Schubert, 53–55
Giotto, 2, 23
Goldoni, Carlo, 12, 13, 14, 15, 86

Haydn, Joseph, 2, 19, 21, 24, 39, 45, 53, 56, 60, 68
Heine, Heinrich, 50
Hildebrand, Dietrich von, xxi, 1n
    Works
        Aesthetics, xxiv, 69n, 70n, 77n, 82n, 95n
        Liturgy and Personality, 28n
        My Battle Against Hitler, xxiii
        "The New Functionalism in the Light of Christ," 2n, 26n
    Phenomenological approach, xxiv
Haecker, Theodor, 1
Handel, George Frideric, 2, 5, 24, 39, 51, 53, 68
Henrici, Christian Friedrich (Picander), 74
Hoffmann, E.T.A., 24
Hofmannsthal, Hugo von, 1, 21–22
Hölderlin, Friedrich, 59

Jesus Christ, 71–76, 93–95
John of the Cross, St. 94

Keats, John, 25
Kierkegaard, Søren, 1–2
Kleist, Heinrich von, 50, 59
Klopstock, Friedrich Gottlieb, 43

Lanner, Joseph, 50
Leonardo da Vinci, 2
Liszt, Franz, 66

Michelangelo, 2, 21, 23, 32, 33, 37, 39, 47
Mahler, Gustav, 81
Molière, 12, 14
Mottl, Felix, 9
Mozart, Leopold, 20
Mozart, Wolfgang Amadeus, xx, xxi, xxii, xxiv, xxv, 1–23, 28, 35–37, 39, 41, 44–45, 51, 53, 61, 68, 71–72, 76–77, 79–83, 87, 99
    Artistic characteristics
        Effortlessness, 4, 16
        Inner necessity, 4, 12, 17
        Joy, 45–46, 64–65
        Universality, 4, 21, 34–35
        Catholic spirit, 20–21
        Misunderstanding of Mozart, 1–3, 10, 14–15
        Sacred music, 17, 20–21
Müller, Wilhelm, 55

Nestroy, Johann, 50
Novalis, 24

Plato, 70
Ponte, Lorenzo da, 7

Raphael, 2, 21, 23
Raymund, Ferdinand, 50
Rossini, Gioachino, 7, 25, 86
Rückert, Friedrich, 55

Schikaneder, Emanuel, 15
Schiller, Friedrich, 24, 27, 55
Schindler, Anton, 65, 67
Schopenhauer, Arthur, 94
Schubert, Franz, 2, 22, 24–25, 36, 39, 43–68, 76, 90, 99, xxiv
    Artistic characteristics
        Charm, 47, 49, 51, 53, 55, 61
        Daemonic [*daemonisch*] power, 47, 61, 64, 66
        Joy, 46, 64–65
        Melancholy, xx, 45, 55
        Poetic quality, 25, 47, 56–57, 61–62

Circle of Friends
   Bauernfeld, Eduard von, 45, 60
   Grillparzer, Franz, 45, 50, 65
   Grün, Anastasius, 45, 50
   Feuchtersleben, Ernst von, 45, 50
   Fröhlich, Kathi, 65
   Hüttenbrenner, Anselm, 45, 50–52, 65, 67
   Kupelwieser, Leopold, 50
   Ottenwalt, Anton, 66
   Schober, Franz von, 45, 50, 58
   Schwind, Moritz von, 45, 51, 66
   Spaun, Joseph von, 43, 45, 58, 65
   Vogl, Johann Michael, 45, 58
   Influence of Beethoven on, 43, 51–52, 67
   Relationship to nature, 48, 56–57
   Sacred music, 6, 64, 76
   Schubertiaden, 45, 50–51, 64
   Tragic element, 45–46, 63–64, 66
Schumann, Robert, 24, 25, 61
Shakespeare, William, 6–9, 15, 23, 51, 53–54, 78, 91, 95–97
   Female characters, 7–8
   Influence on music, 7, 53–54, 95–97
   Shakespearean fashioning of characters, 6, 37, 80
   Works
      As You Like It, 7–9
      Cymbeline, 51
      Hamlet, 91
      Henry IV, 97
      King Lear, 78, 91
      Macbeth, 11, 91
      Othello, 10, 53, 91, 96
      Romeo and Juliet, 78
      The Merchant of Venice, 9
      The Merry Wives of Windsor, 96–97
Stifter, Adalbert, 50
Strauss, Johann, Sr., 50

Teresa of Avila, St., 94
Titian, 2

Uhland, Ludwig, 55
Ulibishev, Alexander, 2

Verdi, Giuseppe, 4–5, 7, 17, 53–54, 76, 83, 95–97
Virgin Mary, 21, 71, 93–94

Wagner, Richard, 4–5, 17, 24–25, 39, 44, 56, 59, 82–97
   Artistic characteristics
      Interpenetration of music and drama, 82–85, 96
      Leitmotif, 83–86, 95
      Through-composition, 83–84, 95
   Bayreuth, xxii, 88
   Connection to Hildebrand family, xxii–xxiii
   Philosophical themes
      Denunciation of power, xxiii
      Glorification of love and compassion, xxiii
Walter, Bruno, 9
Weber, Carl Maria von, 5, 17, 24, 25, 48, 50
Willemer, Marianne von, 54

Index of Musical Works

Bach, Johann Sebastian
   Christmas Oratorio, 69, 75–76
   Mass in B Minor, 76
   St. Matthew Passion, 20, 69, 74–75, 94

Beethoven, Ludwig van
   Egmont Overture, 39
   Fidelio, 5, 10, 27–29, 34, 36–38, 50, 52, 59, 77–81, 90
      Leonore Overture, 38, 79, 81
   Lieder
      Adelaide, 53
      An die ferne Geliebte, 28, 36, 53
      Herz mein Herz, 53
      Ich liebe Dich so wie Du mich, 52
      Kennst du das Land, 53
      Scottish Songs, 36
   Missa solemnis, 2, 21, 27, 34–38, 40, 42, 61, 69, 71, 73, 75, 88, 94
   Piano Concertos, 27, 36
      Fifth Piano Concerto, 34, 38
      Fourth Piano Concerto, 34, 38
   Piano Sonatas, 35–36
      Piano Sonata Opus 26, 38
   String Quartets, 27, 31, 38
      "Harp" Quartet, 33
      Late Quartets, 31, 38
      Quartet Opus 127, 40
      Quartet Opus 130, 34
      Quartet Opus 132, 29, 38
      Cavatina, 33
      Quartet Opus 59 ("Razumovsky"), 31, 34, 38
   Symphonies
      Symphony No. 3 ("Eroica"), 28–29, 33, 38–39
      Symphony No. 4, 34–35, 38
      Symphony No. 5, xx, 33, 35, 38, 46
      Fate Motif, xx
      Symphony No. 6 ("Pastoral"), 34, 38, 46, 90
      Symphony No. 7, 34, 38
      Symphony No. 8, 34
      Symphony No. 9, 2, 12, 25, 29–34, 37–38, 40, 46, 50, 80
   Violin Concerto, 36, 38, 40
Bruckner, Anton
   Mass in F Minor, 76

INDEX OF MUSICAL WORKS

Symphonies, 69
Te Deum, 76

Gluck, Christoph Willibald
Alceste, 77
Iphigénie en Tauride, 5, 51
Orfeo ed Euridice, 5, 80

Mozart, Wolfgang Amadeus
Ave verum corpus, 20–21, 76
Chamber music, 4, 17–19, 51, 61–62
Clarinet Concerto, 19
Clarinet Quintet, 19
Divertimenti, 19
Piano Concerto No. 21, i
Piano Quartets, 19
Quintet in G Minor, 17
Cosí fan tutte, 5, 12–15, 38, 81
Don Giovanni, 5–6, 8–13, 15, 17, 59, 77, 79–81
Laudate Dominum, 21, 76
Mass in C Minor, 20, 61, 69, 71–72
Requiem, 21, 76
Symphonies, 4, 17
G-Minor Symphony (No. 40), 17, 35,
"Haffner" Symphony, 17
"Jupiter" Symphony, 17
"Prague" Symphony, 17
Symphony in E-flat major, 17
The Abduction from the Seraglio, 5–8
The Magic Flute, 5, 15–17, 20, 72, 80–81
The Marriage of Figaro, 5–9, 12, 14–15, 38, 59, 72, 77, 79–81

Rossini, Gioachino
The Barber of Seville, 86

Schubert, Franz
Chamber music, 46, 49, 61–64, 68
B-flat Major Trio, 46, 49, 62–63, 68
C Major Quintet, 46–47, 49, 62–64, 68
"Death and the Maiden" Quartet, 46, 55, 62, 64
Octet, 46, 49, 62–63, 68
Piano Quintet in A major ("Trout Quintet"), 46, 49, 61, i
Quartet Opus 161, 46, 62–63, 68
Quartettsatz, 61
Lieder
Alinde, 46, 56
Am Grabe Anselmos, 55
An Silvia, 46, 49, 54–55
An die Musik, 55
An die Nachtigall, 49
Das Echo, 47
Der Doppelgänger, 55
Der Hirt auf dem Felsen, 49
Der Leiermann, 55–56, 58
Der Lindenbaum, 47, 55, 58
Der Tod und das Mädchen, 55, 62
Der Wanderer, 46
Der Wegweiser, 55, 58
Die Allmacht, 67
Die Forelle, 51, 55
Die Krähe, 55
Die Nachtigall, 56
Die junge Nonne, 67
Die schöne Müllerin, 49, 57–58, 67
Ich hört' ein Bächlein rauschen, 56
Du bist die Ruh, 55
Erlkönig, 44, 47, 54–56, 60, 64
Ganymed, 49, 54–55
Grenzen der Menschheit, 67
Gretchen am Spinnrad, 44, 46, 53–55, 57, 60
Gruppe aus dem Tartarus, 47, 49, 51, 55
Heidenröslein, 47, 55
Horch, horch die Lerch' im Ätherblau, 51

INDEX OF MUSICAL WORKS

Im Dorfe, 58
Im Grünen, 49
Iphigenia's Monologue, 67
Sehnsucht, 49, 55
Suleika, 47, 49, 51, 54–55
Suleikas Erster Gesang, 54
Viola, 67
Winterreise, 46, 57–58
Der Leiermann, 55–56, 58
Der Wegweiser, 55, 58
Die Krähe, 55
Im Dorfe, 58
Mass in E-flat Major, 61, 64, 76
Piano Sonatas, 49
Rosamunde, 49, 60
Symphonies
Symphony No. 1, 60
Symphony No. 2, 60
Symphony No. 3, 60
Symphony No. 4 ("Tragic"), 60
Symphony No. 5, 60
Symphony No. 6, 60
Symphony in B Minor ("Unfinished"), 51, 60, i
Symphony in C Major, 47, 49, 51, 60, 64

Schumann, Robert
Traumerei

Verdi, Giuseppe
Falstaff, 5, 95–97
La Traviata, 83
Otello, 5, 53, 95–96
Requiem, 76, 95
Rigoletto, 83

Wagner, Richard
Das Rheingold, 83, 86, 88
Die Meistersinger, 5, 59, 85
Lohengrin, 83, 85, 91, 94
Parsifal, 83, 91, 94
Ring cycle, 84, 91
Tannhäuser, 83, 91–94
The Flying Dutchman, 82–85
Tristan und Isolde, 5, 59, 85–86, 90, 93–94

Weber, Carl Maria von
Der Freischütz, 11, 25, 48
Euryanthe, 49–50
Oberon, 49

www.ingramcontent.com/pod-product-compliance
Lightning Source LLC
Chambersburg PA
CBHW062113080426
42734CB00012B/2848